Has the West Lost It?

Has the West Lost It?

A Provocation

KISHORE MAHBUBANI

ALLEN LANE
an imprint of
PENGUIN BOOKS

ALLEN LANE

UK | USA | Canada | Ireland | Australia
India | New Zealand | South Africa

Allen Lane is part of the Penguin Random House group of companies whose
addresses can be found at global.penguinrandomhouse.com

Penguin
Random House
UK

First published 2018
001

Copyright © Kishore Mahbubani, 2018

The moral right of the author has been asserted

Set in 12.8/15.2 pt Garamond MT Std
Typeset by Jouve (UK), Milton Keynes
Printed at Thomson Press India Ltd, New Delhi

A CIP catalogue record for this book is available from the British Library

ISBN: 978–0–241–31286–5

. . . there is nothing more difficult to take in hand, more perilous to conduct, or more uncertain in its success, than to take the lead in the introduction of a new order of things.

Niccolò Machiavelli, *The Prince*, Chapter VI

Has the West Lost It?

A New Order of Things

Why is the West feeling lost? The answer is simple. In the early twenty-first century, history has turned a corner, perhaps the most significant corner humanity has ever turned – yet the West refuses to accept or adapt to this new historical era.

What is this big turn that history has taken? A brief comparison of the past 200 years with the previous 1,800 years will provide the answer. From AD 1 to 1820, the two largest economies were always those of China and India. Only after that period did Europe take off, followed by America. Viewed against the backdrop of the past 1,800 years, the recent period of Western relative over-performance against other civilizations is a major historical aberration. All such aberrations come to a natural end, and that is happening now.

So what is the problem? It is important to understand the nature of our times. The strategist Machiavelli emphasized this when he said: 'The prince who relies entirely on fortune is lost when it changes. I believe also that he will be successful who directs his actions according to the spirit of the times, and that he whose actions do not accord with the times will not be successful.'[1]

Yet, even though the spirit of the times has changed, and even though the West will inevitably have to make major adjustments to adapt to this new era, no major Western figure has had the courage to state the defining truth of our times: that a cycle of Western domination of the world is coming to a natural end. Their populations, on the other hand, can feel these large changes in their bones, and in the job markets. This, in part, explains supposedly politically aberrant – to the elites at least – events like Trump and Brexit.

To reveal to their people the scale and speed of the changes, Western leaders should show the two charts below simultaneously. The frequently cited McKinsey chart (Figure 1) shows how long China and India were the world's largest economies, as well as their sudden precipitous drop after 1820. The second chart (Figure 2), highlighted by commentator Martin Wolf, shows how China and India have regained their natural share as those of America and Europe have begun to shrink.

The Western share of the global economy will continue to shrink. This is inevitable and unstoppable, as other societies have learnt to emulate Western best practices. Does this mean that Western livelihoods are bound to get worse? The recent stagnation of incomes and rising job losses among the working classes in America and elsewhere seems to suggest that hard times are coming. R. W. Johnson describes well how wages have stagnated:

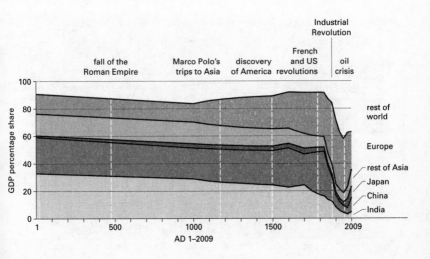

Figure 1. Share of total world GDP[2]

Between 1948 and 1973, productivity rose by 96.7 per cent and real wages by 91.3 per cent, almost exactly in step. Those were the days of plentiful hard-hat jobs in steel and the auto industry when workers could afford to send their children to college and see them rise into the middle class. But from 1973 to 2015 – the era of globalization, when many of those jobs vanished abroad – productivity rose 73.4 per cent while wages rose by only 11.1 per cent.

He also wrote, 'On average in 1965 an American CEO earned 20 times what a worker did. By 2013, on average, the number was 296 times.'[3]

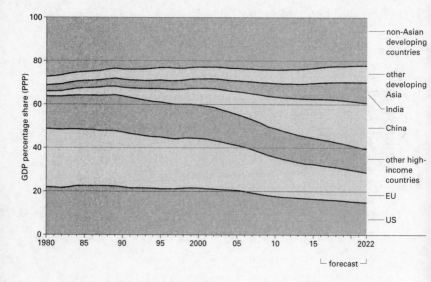

Figure 2. The changing shape of the world economy[4]

The incomes of many Western middle-class populations have also stagnated in recent decades. This is undeniable. But this trend can be reversed. Western leaders need to do a shrewd recalculation of the new global economic order and look for new opportunities for Western workers. As Machiavelli famously warned, 'there is nothing more difficult . . . than to take the lead in the introduction of a new order of things.'

The good news for the West is that the global economic pie is not shrinking. In fact, it is growing steadily,

6

and will probably continue growing – with some significant changes. Until recently, much of global growth came from G7 economies, not the E7 economies.* This has reversed sharply in the past two decades. In 2015, for example, the G7 contributed 31.5 per cent and the E7 36.3 per cent of global growth.

In short, the West has hitherto provided the locomotive driving global economic growth, and the Rest hitched their wagons to the train. China's explosive growth in recent decades was fuelled by exports to America. Now, the Rest are providing the locomotive, and Western societies can deliver economic growth to their populations by hitching their wagons to the Rest.

This sounds simple in theory. In practice, it could be difficult. The West has been at the forefront of world history for almost 200 years. Now it has to learn to share, even abandon, that position and adapt to a world it can no longer dominate. Can this be done? So far, the West has failed to produce a coherent and competitive global strategy to deal with the new situation. Instead, it is flailing about, attacking Iraq, bombing Syria, sanctioning Russia and baiting China. All this adds to a sense of global turbulence.

The key message of this book is that there is a better

---

* G7 = the Group of 7: Canada, France, Germany, Italy, Japan, the UK and the US. E7 = the Emerging 7: China, India, Brazil, Mexico, Russia, Indonesia and Turkey.

option for the West, helped by analysis and advice, offered in friendship, from the Rest. A cold, careful and comprehensive calculation of how Western interests have changed, coupled with ruthless realism – indeed, a dose of Machiavelli – is what the West needs. However, Machiavelli remains also one of the most misunderstood figures of our time. Many in the West regard Machiavelli as the embodiment of evil. Leo Strauss, the famous American political scientist of the 1950s, called him a 'teacher of evil'.[5] In fact, as the great British philosopher Isaiah Berlin reminded us in his seminal essay 'The Question of Machiavelli',[6] 'Machiavelli's values . . . are not instrumental but moral and ultimate, and he calls for great sacrifices in their name.' Berlin stressed that the West's derision for Machiavelli is derived from a 'deep but characteristic misunderstanding of Machiavelli's thesis'. As he explains, Machiavelli understands that 'public life has its own morality'. In other words, Machiavelli advocates that a leader who makes him- or herself 'responsible for the lives of others' has to place their welfare first. A Machiavellian leader must thus always choose pragmatic morals over idealistic or dogmatic ones.

Happily, the West need not make any 'great sacrifices' today, because the state of humankind is far better than it was in sixteenth-century Italy. Although Western populations have been grappling with pessimism recently, a new dawn has broken over the rest of the world. Paradoxically, much of this has happened as a result of the

West sharing its wisdom with the Rest. Sadly, the West remains remarkably ill-informed about the massive improvement in the human condition.

Imagine a world where virtually no human being goes to bed feeling hungry. Or where absolute poverty has all but disappeared. Where every child gets vaccinated and goes to school. Where every home has electricity. Where every human being carries some kind of smartphone, giving him or her uninterrupted access to global treasure troves of information that were once the exclusive preserves of small elites. Most importantly, imagine a world where the prospects of a major world war are practically zero.

Most sensible people would describe such a world as bordering on utopia. Astonishingly few sensible people are aware that we live in a world where humanity is standing on the verge of achieving such a utopia. It's the biggest truth of our times: in objective terms, the human condition has never been better.

Violence has fallen dramatically. Harvard's Steven Pinker observes that '. . . today we are probably living in the most peaceful moment of our species' time on earth.'[7] He adds: 'Global violence has fallen steadily since the middle of the twentieth century. According to the Human Security Brief 2006, the number of battle deaths in interstate wars has declined from more than 65,000 per year in the 1950s to less than 2,000 per year in this decade.'[8] Similarly, poverty has also declined dramatically. Oxford's Max Roser says, 'In 1950 three-quarters of the world were living in extreme poverty; in 1981 it was still 44 per cent. For last year [2016], the research suggests that the share in extreme poverty has fallen below 10 per cent.' On literacy, he says, 'In 1800 there were 120 million people in the world that could read and write; today there are 6.2 billion with the same skill.'[9] Dr Peter Diamandis, the co-founder of Silicon Valley's Singularity University, has concluded, 'We truly are living in the most exciting time to be alive!'[10] Why? He documents how absolute poverty is disappearing, child labour is declining, infant mortality rates are falling, homicide rates are falling and average education and literacy rates are exploding all over the world.

Johan Norberg of the Cato Institute notes: 'If someone had told you in 1990 that over the next twenty-five years world hunger would decline by 40 per cent, child mortality would halve, and extreme poverty would fall by three quarters, you'd have told them they were a naive fool. But the fools were right. This is truly what has happened.'[11] Having experienced Third World poverty as a child, I know that nothing drags down the human spirit more than a sense of helplessness, uncertainty and fear of the future. A small regular income and access to basic goods like TV sets and refrigerators also improves one's sense of well-being. In short, the eradication of poverty is spiritually uplifting. The world should rejoice at this change.

The Gift of Western Wisdom

This enormous improvement in the human condition is a result of a slow process of Western ideas and best practices seeping into other societies. The biggest gift the West gave the Rest was the power of reasoning.

'Reasoning' is a commonly used word. The *Oxford English Dictionary* defines it thus: 'To think (something) through, work out in a logical manner'. Western forms of reasoning have seeped into Asian minds gradually, through the adoption of Western science and technology and the application of the scientific method to solving social problems. Science and technology showed the power of empirical proof and constant verification. It led to the adoption of many new technologies, from modern medicine to electricity, from railways to cell phones, all of which improved lives significantly. The application of the scientific method also provided solutions for the seemingly insoluble problems Asians had experienced for millennia, including floods and famines, pandemics and poverty. Similarly, individuals also began to understand how reasoning could improve their personal sense of well-being. As Bertrand Russell said, 'The world of pure reason knows no compromise, no practical limitations, no barrier to the creative activity embodying in splendid edifices the passionate aspiration after the perfect from which all great work springs.'[12] It did not go directly from the West to all other societies. East Asian societies, especially Japan and the 'Four Tigers' (South Korea, Taiwan, Hong Kong and Singapore), were the first to absorb these ideas and practices, such as free market economics and empirical scientific research. Their success in turn inspired other societies. East Asia provided the first bridge between the West and the Rest.

As the spirit of Western reasoning seeped into Asian societies, it led to the soaring of ambition which, in turn, has generated the many Asian miracles we see unfolding today. It is also leading to success in Estonia, Botswana and Chile, three countries on three different continents.

This spread of Western reasoning, in turn, triggered three silent revolutions that explain the extraordinary success of many non-Western societies in recent decades. These silent revolutions have gone unnoticed in Western intellectual circles.

The first revolution is political. For millennia, Asian societies were deeply feudal. The people were accountable to their rulers, not rulers to their people. 'Oriental despotism' was a fair description of the political environments in all corners of Asia, from Teheran to Tokyo. Each person in Asian societies was supposed to know his or her place. India carried it to the extreme with its caste system. A person's destiny was determined at birth. There was no escape.

The rebellion against all kinds of feudal mind-sets which gained momentum in the second half of the twentieth century was hugely liberating for all Asian societies. Millions of Asians went from being passive bystanders to becoming active agents of change. They took control of their personal destinies. Over time, the rulers of most Asian societies came to understand and accept that they were accountable to their people, not the people to them. These changes could be clearly seen in those societies that accepted democratic forms of government, like India and Japan, South Korea and Sri Lanka. However, an equally profound political revolution was taking place in the non-democratic societies.

This explains the extraordinary success of China over the past four decades. In theory, there was no change when China went from being ruled by one Communist Party leader, Mao Zedong, to another, Deng Xiaoping. In practice, a fundamental political revolution took place. Mao behaved exactly like a traditional Chinese emperor, issuing edicts that often caused great human suffering. By contrast, Deng focused all his energies on improving the living conditions of the Chinese people. He educated them enormously. He opened the world to them. In so doing, he completely changed the social contract between the

Chinese Communist Party and the Chinese people. All of Deng's successors – Jiang Zemin, Hu Jintao and Xi Jinping – know that, at the end of the day, they are accountable to the people. This explains the extraordinary transformation of Chinese society. 800 million Chinese have been rescued from absolute poverty in three decades.

This is also why many Asian countries, including hitherto troubled countries like Burma (Myanmar) and Bangladesh, Pakistan and the Philippines, are progressing slowly and steadily. In each of these four countries, various forms of dictatorship have been replaced by leaders who believe that they are accountable to their populations. Many of their troubles continue, but poverty has diminished significantly, the middle classes are growing and modern education is spreading. There are no perfect democracies in Asia (and, as we have learned after Trump and Brexit, democracies in the West are deficient, too). In theory, democratic processes are designed to deliver results that reflect the will of the people. Also, since each citizen is entitled to participate in the processes, the result should be accepted by all and result in national consensus building. Instead, democratic processes in the US and the UK have recently led to deep polarization, with virtual civil wars continuing even after election and referendum results have come in. Western theorists of democracy need to go back to their drawing boards to figure out where democratic processes have gone awry. In Asia, a different story is evolving. The political systems remain hugely imperfect. However, in a big shift from previous 'despotic' assumptions, most Asian leaders now recognize that they are accountable to their people, and as long as they have to demonstrate daily that they are improving their people's lives Asian societies will continue to improve. This is one big gift that Western reasoning has made to Asia.

Today, Africans and Latin Americans are learning from Asian success stories. In 2008, Kenya launched Vision 2030, an ambitious development programme that was heavily inspired by similar concepts in Singapore and Malaysia.[13] Kenya's northern neighbour, Ethiopia, has been explicit in its admiration and emulation of South Korea and Taiwan.[14] In 2015, Ethiopian President Mulatu Teshome said, 'Ethiopia is going through a national renaissance, following Korea's model of development.'[15] The World Bank's South-South Knowledge Exchange Initiative has fostered the exchange of policy lessons and technical assistance between Latin American countries and their developing Asian counterparts. Costa Rica's Investment Promotion Agency, CINDE, followed Singapore's best practice and persuaded Intel to establish a processing plant in the country.[16]

The second revolution is psychological: the Rest are going from believing that they were helpless voyagers in a life determined by 'fate' to believing that they can take control of their lives and rationally produce better outcomes. In my lifetime, we have gone from my parents' generation, who had zero university education, to my children's generation, who are experiencing almost universal university education. Now multiply these experiences millions, if not hundreds of millions, of times. In the last thirty years, we have carried more people over the threshold of university education than we have in the previous 3,000 years.

It makes a huge difference if you believe that you can create a better life for yourself and your children. Billions more people believe that they can do this. This enormous psychological revolution also explains why the human condition is getting better.

The third revolution is in the field of governance. Here, too, the major transformation can be seen most acutely in Asia. Fifty years ago, few Asian governments believed that good rational governance could transform their societies. Now most do.

Take the case of Asia's three most populous countries: China, India and Indonesia. All three had strong founding leaders in the post-colonial era: Mao Zedong, Jawaharlal Nehru and Sukarno. They were very different personalities, but they shared one common trait: they focused on politics, not governance. This may be because the personality required to lead a country through a revolution or a struggle for political freedom is not necessarily that of someone who knows how to govern and administer a newly established nation state. Even the great soul Nelson Mandela struggled to provide good governance.

By contrast, the current leaders, Xi Jinping, Narendra Modi and Jokowi (who are also very different in personality) share a common conviction that good governance will transform and uplift their societies. They are actively searching out and implementing public policies that could put their countries on a secure long-term road of economic development. All three also have severe political challenges to deal with domestically, yet all three are equally determined that this should not prevent them from delivering good governance to their societies. Modi is often criticized in the Western media for his right-wing nationalist stances. Some of these political stances are tactical moves, to gain stronger political support. In many elections, he has received broad-based support from all ethnic and religious groups, including Muslims.

This recent experience of rational good governance, in the form of beneficial public policies, may also explain why the populations of China, India and Indonesia are more optimistic than their counterparts in the West. According to a study by Populus in 2016, 90 per cent of young Indonesians said that they were happy, compared to just 57 per cent in Britain and France. According to the same study, the countries with the highest proportions of young people who think the world is getting better are China, India and Nigeria. In China, India and Indonesia, more than 90 per cent of young people named technology as the factor that made them most hopeful for the future.[17]

Suicidal Western Wars

In the field of governance, we are witnessing a paradox. Asians learnt the virtues of rational governance from the West. Yet, many Western populations are losing their trust in governance, while Asian levels of trust are increasing. According to the Government at a Glance 2013 survey conducted by Gallup, India ranked second in trust in national government among the countries surveyed. An OECD Report based on the survey said that 'Trust in government in all BRIICS [Brazil, Russia, India, Indonesia, China, South Africa] countries was higher than the OECD average (40 per cent).'[18]

This rising belief in rational governance is happening not just in Asia. It is happening in Africa too. During the Cold War, America strongly supported strongman rulers like President Mobutu of Zaire, who did little but fleece their countries. By contrast, many strongman rulers in Africa today are focused on rational governance of their societies. This is why President Yoweri Museveni of Uganda and President Paul Kagame of Rwanda have delivered remarkable economic and social development to their countries. From 1990 to 2015, life expectancy improved significantly – from 45 to 58 in Uganda and from 33 to 64 in Rwanda. The infant mortality rate* decreased from 111.4 per 1,000 live births in 1990 to 37.7 in Uganda and from 93.2 to 31.1 in Rwanda.

But the Rest have not sent a 'thank you' note to the West. Initially – indeed, for centuries – the West used its military and technological prowess to conquer and dominate the planet. Modern science and technology were harnessed to create powerful weapons. By the end of the nineteenth century, Western power had exploded into every part of the planet. Virtually every society on Earth – including the two previously greatest economic powers, China and India (which had almost half of the world's GDP in 1820[19]) – was subjugated by the West. Every other human civilization had no choice but to bend before Western power. And this domination could have carried on for many more centuries if not for the two suicidal world wars which the Western powers indulged in in the first half of the twentieth century.

These wars, and the rejuvenation of non-Western societies using Western best practices, explain the political liberation of the rest of the world from Western domination in the second half of the twentieth century. This liberation was visible in the new flags flying all

---

* Infant mortality rate is defined as the probability of dying between birth and exactly one year of age expressed per 1,000 live births.

over the world. What was not visible was the real intellectual liberation that came more slowly and only gathered pace towards the end of the twentieth century. It took a few decades, but the rest of the world eventually figured out how they could replicate Western success stories in economic growth, health, education, and so forth.

The West either didn't notice or didn't care. Why not? This liberation of billions of non-Western minds coincided with another moment of Western triumphalism: the end of the Cold War. Moments of triumphalism are inherently dangerous. The giddy spirits of the West were ready to ingest any form of seductive opium. Conveniently, they found this in Francis Fukuyama's famous essay 'The End of History?' In it, he boldly argued: 'What we may be witnessing is not just the end of the Cold War, or the passing of a particular period of post-war history, but the end of history as such: that is, the end point of mankind's ideological evolution and the universalization of Western liberal democracy as the final form of human government.'[20] Western rulers fell in love with his essay and began to believe that their societies had reached the top of the metaphorical Mount Everest of human development and would not be dislodged.

Partly as a result of imbibing Fukuyama's opiate, triumphalists in the West didn't notice that the end of the Cold War coincided with a more fundamental turn of human history, which triggered a new historical era rather than ending history. China and India – the two sleeping giants of Asia – were waking up. Deng Xiaoping's Four Modernizations policy – reforming the fields of agriculture, industry, national defence and science and technology – gathered pace in the 1980s. Prime Minister Narasimha Rao opened up the Indian economy in 1991, ushering in foreign investment, reducing import tariffs and duties and deregulating markets.

The sound of the Western celebratory drums at the end of the Cold War was not the only event hiding the return of China as a major player in the international order. The Tiananmen Square events happened in June 1989. The mass demonstrations and the killings that followed convinced the West that the Chinese communist regime was another corrupt regime about to collapse. As a result, the West didn't notice the remarkably bold decision of Deng Xiaoping to carry on with the opening of the Chinese economy despite the huge political challenge posed by Tiananmen. A more nervous Chinese leader would have shuttered China again. Deng didn't. As a result, Chinese economic growth continued steadily in the 1990s. This gave China the confidence to apply to join the World Trade Organization (WTO).

Then another event distracted the West: 9/11, in 2001. Instead of reacting thoughtfully and intelligently, the prevailing intellectual hubris led to the disastrous decision to invade Iraq. America has the world's best universities and think tanks, as well as the most globally influential professors and pundits, yet none of them highlighted or highlight now the fact that the most historically consequential event in 2001 was not 9/11. It was China's entry into the WTO. The entry of almost a billion workers into the global trading system would obviously result in massive 'creative destruction' and the loss of many jobs in the West. In August 2017, a Bank for International Settlements report confirmed that the introduction of new workers from China and Eastern Europe led to 'declining real wages and a smaller share of labour in national output'. It added that this 'naturally meant that inequality [within Western economies] rose'.[21]

This was one major reason why Trump and Brexit happened fifteen years later. The working-class populations could feel directly what their elites couldn't. Their lives were being disrupted by fundamental changes taking place in the world order, and their leaders had done nothing to explain to them what was happening, or to mitigate the damage. Sadly, most elites in the West still view with contempt all those who voted in favour of Trump and Brexit. Hillary Clinton revealed this when she described Trump's supporters as a 'basket of deplorables'.

The Blindness of Western Elites

Western elites, who remain the most globally influential elites, believe that they understand the world better than anyone else. They display little humility when they write in the pages of the *New York Times* or the *Financial Times*, the *Wall Street Journal* or the *Economist*, or when they speak on the BBC and CNN. Most of these elites remain convinced that they are right. Yet they are now distrusted by their masses, who sense in their daily lives the emergence of a new world that the elites either pretend is not happening or dismiss.

These Western elites need to develop a good understanding of this new era that is emerging forcefully, and work with their own populations to formulate thoughtful and pragmatic policy responses that will help everyone prepare for the great changes that have begun, and which will only gain further momentum through the twenty-first century. Adapting to great change is never easy, especially when this massive return of the Rest is coinciding with several other structural revolutions. The world of 2050 will bear little resemblance to the world of 1950, or even 2000. To understand why, just look at Figure 3.

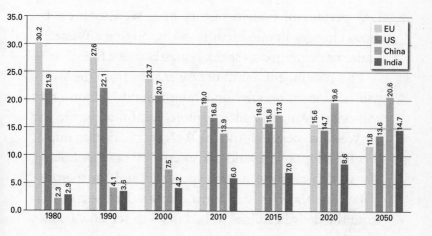

Figure 3. Percentage share of world GDP to 2050[22]

In 1976, the West launched the G7 to bring together the world's most powerful economies. Their share of the global GDP was 45.3 per cent in 1995.[23] By contrast, the share of the E7, the seven largest emerging economies, then was half that at 22.6 per cent. However, by 2015 their respective shares were 31.5 per cent (G7) and 36.3 per cent (E7). PricewaterhouseCoopers has forecast that by 2050, the G7 share will slide to 20 per cent and that of the E7 will have risen to almost 50 per cent in purchasing power parity (PPP) terms.*[24]

*Economic indicators expressed in PPP terms are more valid for international comparisons. This is because PPP-based metrics

Few periods of human history have seen such enormous changes in one lifetime. Sadly, no brave Western leader has emerged to speak honestly about them.

This monumental shift of power away from the West will be uncomfortable for Western minds. Ignoring it will only mean delayed and more painful adjustments for Western societies. And the West should bear in mind that the adoption of various Western best practices globally is also creating a more peaceful and prosperous planet that the West can live in happily. Let's step back from the daily headlines of bad news to see how countries that were seen as hopeless are progressing.

Pakistan is one of the most troubled countries in the world. Virtually no one sees Pakistan as a symbol of hope. Yet, despite being thrust into the frontlines by George W. Bush after 9/11 in 2001 and forced to join the battle against the Taliban, 'Pakistan experienced a "staggering fall" in poverty from 2002 to 2014, according to the World Bank, halving to 29.5 per cent of the population.'[25] In the same period, the middle-class population soared.

Henry Kissinger famously described Bangladesh as a 'basket case' country after he opposed the separation

---

take into account the differences in cost of living and inflation in the respective countries. PPP is calculated using a 'basket of goods' approach. Using this method, two currencies will have the same value if a predetermined basket of goods is priced the same in both their countries.

of Bangladesh from Pakistan in 1971. Yet it has achieved an average rate of 5.5 per cent growth over the past two decades.[26] More amazingly, the World Bank has announced that Bangladesh can reach its goal of achieving 'middle income' status by 2021. Life expectancy in Bangladesh has also risen sharply, from 45.83 in 1960 to 69.68 in 2010. For the first time in centuries, the poor people of Bangladesh are feeling hopeful for the future. Hope begets happiness.

When countries like Bangladesh and Pakistan have begun marching steadily towards middle-class status for a significant part of their populations, the world has turned a corner. Indeed, the statistics for the growth of middle classes globally are staggering. From a base of 1.8 billion in 2009, the number will hit 3.2 billion by 2020. By 2030, the number will hit 4.9 billion,[27] which means that more than half the world's population will enjoy middle-class living standards by then.

In theory, these statistics only tell a story about economic development. In practice, these statistics are about the elimination of human suffering and a daily increase in the sum of human happiness. As a result of economic growth, each year new clinics and schools are built; electricity lines and water pipes are laid; more children are vaccinated; women get educated; fewer babies die; more people live longer; and people get better jobs. In short, all the things that Western populations took for granted and the Rest thought were out of their grasp are becoming universal. For the majority of us, the past three decades – 1990 to 2020 – have been the best in human history.

A happier humanity is emerging. It's not an exaggeration to say that we may be on the verge of utopia. Why have we not begun to celebrate this? One possible reason is that we have become addicted to 'news'. We pay attention to events, not trends. One good case study is provided by Malaysia. Many well-informed observers of Malaysia are aware of the many trials and tribulations Malaysia has suffered in the past three decades: the spectacular political clash between Dr Mahathir and his deputy PM Anwar Ibrahim in 1997, resulting in Anwar Ibrahim's beating and imprisonment; Dr Mahathir's successful campaign to unseat his successor, Abdullah Badawi, in 2003; and the ongoing – so far unsuccessful – campaign to unseat the current PM, Najib Razak. Foreign observers are also aware of the Malaysian Airlines (MAS) plane MH 17, shot down in Ukraine on 17 July 2014, and MH 370, which is still missing after disappearing on 8 March 2014. Malaysia is also associated with the scandals surrounding the 1Malaysia Development Berhad (where close associates of Prime Minister Najib Razak were implicated in financial improprieties[28]) and the dramatic killing of the brother of the North Korean leader at the Kuala Lumpur airport on 13 February 2017. Malaysia has had more than its fair share of bad news.

As a result, few people are aware that, in terms of human development, Malaysia is one of the most successful countries in the developing world. Its poverty rate has gone down spectacularly from 51.2 per cent in 1958[29] to 1.7 per cent in 2012.[30] Its middle class grew by 6.5 million people from 1990 to 2008.[31] According to a 2015 study by the Pew Research Center, Malaysia experienced the greatest increase in the share of the population that are upper-middle-class income earners, which rose from 12 per cent in 2001 to 29 per cent in 2011. According to a study by NYU,[32] in 1967, there were 25 vehicles per 1,000 members of the population in Malaysia. By 2002, this number had grown to 240 vehicles per 1,000.

Similarly, Internet penetration rates rose from 21.4 per cent in 2000 to 68.6 per cent in 2016. Smartphone penetration rose from 51 per cent in 2014 to 71 per cent in 2016. According to the spring 2015 Pew Global Attitudes survey, which measured the share of adults owning a smartphone, Malaysia ranked ninth in the world. As a result, Malaysians have become well-connected with the new modern economy.

This ignorance about the extraordinary progress made by billions on our planet is aggravated by the global supremacy of Western media, which dominate global news and infect the world with the prevailing Western pessimism.

Historians in the future will marvel at how the end of the 200-year Western domination of world history *circa* 2020 coincided with a new dawn in human history. It could have been otherwise. The end of Western domination could have resulted in a new dark age for the world. Indeed, many in the West still believe that we are on the threshold of such a dark age today. The truth is the exact opposite.

Given the dominance of bad news in the West, accentuated by Trump and Brexit, few in the West have noticed another startling fact of our times. Three of the four most populous countries in our world are Asian: China (1.3 billion), India (1.2 billion) and Indonesia (250 million). All three are led by exceptionally honest and competent leaders: Xi Jinping, Narendra Modi and Jokowi, respectively. Is this an amazing coincidence? Or is it, perhaps, a reflection of our times? These societies are in the throes of a new resurgence. As such, their people expect and support strong, competent leaders.

Xi, Modi and Jokowi are exceptionally competent. However, they are not exceptional in providing relatively good governance. As indicated earlier, more and more countries are enjoying functional, instead of dysfunctional, governance. Functional governance is good enough to improve the lives of people and lift living standards. Today, most governments of the world have become functional.

Why is this not studied or discussed? At least in part it is because the media only cover the more dysfunctional governments. A region-by-region analysis would show that every region in the world enjoys more functional than dysfunctional governments. Southeast Asia was a hotbed of conflict and strife from 1945 to 1985. Now, as Jeffery Sng and I document in our book *The ASEAN Miracle*, all ten ASEAN governments are functional and thrusting Southeast Asia forward to become the fourth-largest economic area in the world by 2050.

No other region can show such a sharp contrast between its dysfunctional past and its functional future, but Southeast Asia is not an exception. South Asia, another strife-ridden area, now probably has only one dysfunctional government, Nepal. As documented earlier, even Pakistan and Bangladesh are progressing slowly and steadily. In the neighbouring Gulf region, the news focuses on the conflict in Yemen. Yet, next door to Yemen, another nation, Oman, has been gradually making progress for decades. Oman's per capita GDP has increased from US $9,907 in 1980 to US $15,965 in 2015.[33] Indeed, most members of the Gulf Cooperation Council are doing well. One leading indicator to watch is the percentage of women being educated. In Saudi Arabia alone, female tertiary enrolment rose from 10.7 per cent in 1991 to 59.8 per cent in 2014.[34] In a huge breakthrough, in September 2017 the Saudi king finally lifted the ban on women drivers. Modernity is seeping into all corners of the world.

Latin American governments have also become

more functional. Venezuela stands out as an exception. Similarly, overall Sub-Saharan Africa is making steady progress. For every Somalia that is dysfunctional, there are several neighbours that are functional, including Ethiopia, Djibouti, Kenya and Tanzania. Ethiopia was long a symbol of African poverty. However, its per capita income has increased by 214 per cent in the past three decades.[35] Rwanda and Uganda have also grown their per capita income in a sustainable way.

By a curious coincidence, the two regions that seem to be an exception to this broad trend are the two regions that the West has meddled in the most in recent times: North Africa and the Middle East. Is the relative failure of these two regions a result of bad luck? Poor leadership? Flawed societies and cultures? Or Western meddling?

Twenty-five years ago, I warned Europe that if it didn't take better care of North Africa, boatloads of refugees would cross the tiny sea that is the Mediterranean. I wrote,

If something goes wrong in, say, Algeria or Tunisia, the problems will impact on France. In the eyes of the North African population, the Mediterranean, which once divided civilizations, has become a mere pond. What human being would not cross a pond if thereby he could improve his livelihood? Through all previous centuries, men and women have crossed oceans and mountains to seek a better life, often suffering terrible hardship in the process.[36]

It didn't take a strategic genius to see this coming. Yet Europeans were shocked when refugees began to arrive from North Africa.

It is therefore vital to stress here that the stories from North Africa and the Middle East (especially Iraq and Syria) that hog Western newspaper headlines are the sharp exception to a larger global surge of functional governance. As the Dean of a School of Public Policy, I saw daily how the appetite and capacity for functional governance has spread globally.

The Global Explosion of Travel

Functional governance can improve people's living standards significantly in a lifetime. By the rule of 72,* if a country grows at 5 per cent a year (and many developing countries are achieving this rate of growth), a country's per capita income doubles every fourteen years. Hence, in the next thirty years, if most of the states grow at this rate (and the three most populous states – China, India and Indonesia – are at least likely to do so), the standard of living of a vast majority of humanity will quadruple in the next thirty years. This statistic, more than anything else, should occupy the thoughts and approaches of governments and rulers around the world.

We can see the impact of higher living standards in the global explosion of travel beyond borders. A popular Western expression is 'people vote with their feet'. More and more people are voting with their feet nowadays. They are voting with their feet to travel overseas. And they are also voting with their feet to return home.

*The 'rule of 72' is a shortcut formula by which: years required to double an investment = 72 divided by the annual interest rate.

These are the global figures. In 1950, the world saw 25.3 million international tourist arrivals.[37] In 2015, the number had hit 1.16 billion – a 45-fold increase. The current projection is that by 2030, thirteen years from now, the number could hit 1.8 billion.[38]

International tourism is the ultimate luxury. You have to ensure that you have taken care of all your immediate needs and the foreseeable needs of your family before you can afford to spend a significant amount of money on international travel. Airfares and hotels are not necessarily cheap, but they are getting progressively cheaper in the era of budget airlines and Airbnb. After you have saved enough money for travel, you want to travel to safe places. Clearly, Afghanistan and Syria are not going to get tourists for a while.

A common refrain of Western leaders is that the world is a dangerous place. George W. Bush said in 2006, 'The American people need to know we live in a dangerous world.' Ten years have passed since he said this. If he had been right, we should have seen a sharp reduction in international tourist flows over the past decade, especially since tourists tend to be risk-averse. They do not travel overseas to endanger their lives. Yet in the period 2005 to 2014, while the world was ostensibly getting more dangerous, the number of international tourists jumped from 823 million to 1.16 billion.[39]

The story of tourist flows from China is particularly telling. The Chinese are voting with their feet in ever greater numbers. In 1980, when I first visited China, there were zero Chinese tourists going overseas. Only officials travelled overseas. By 2015, there were 100 million Chinese tourists. Why is this figure remarkable? Many in the West still see the Chinese people as suffering because they are ruled by a repressive and harsh communist regime. If this Western perception were true, would 100 million Chinese people be able to travel overseas freely? (The old Soviet Union, also run by a communist party, never allowed Soviet citizens to travel overseas.) And more significantly, would 100 million Chinese tourists return home freely if they were indeed oppressed? The inability to see the explosion of new personal freedoms that the Chinese people are enjoying means that the West is also unable to see that Chinese civilization is beginning to experience the most glorious period ever in its 3,000-year history.

A similar renaissance will occur in many societies as we become a world with universal access to information. As a young poor boy in Singapore in the 1950s, I wanted to own the *Encyclopaedia Britannica*. I never fulfilled this dream. Today, most young boys and girls will eventually get access to the contents of an equivalent of the *Encyclopaedia Britannica*. Sometime in the next decade or two, we will live in a world where over half the world's population will have access to a smartphone, and smartphones are getting smarter and smarter. As recently as 1990, there were close to zero mobile phones in India.[40] By December 2015, there were almost a billion subscriptions, though most of them were for 'dumb' phones.[41] Today, India is the world's second-largest smartphone market, with more than 220 million unique users.[42] According to the 2016 Ericsson Mobility Report, Indian usage is predicted to nearly quadruple to reach 810 million smartphone subscriptions by 2021.[43] That is only three years away.

Just as India took a major leapfrog over landlines to provide universal access to all phones, it will take another major leapfrog over ATMs to create a cashless society by enabling smartphones to make payments. China is already ahead of America and Europe in doing this. Many of life's little inconveniences disappear with the smartphone. The smartphone also helps explain why we are experiencing the greatest advancements of the human condition: leapfrog technology is a critical ingredient.

Future generations will also identify another critical historical turning point in our time: the information revolution. For most of human history, access to education and information was limited to small groups of elites. Now it has become almost universalized, as primary education is reaching each child. All this is also spreading the culture of modern reasoning gifted by the West. With functional governance, reasoning and smarter, more comfortable populations, wars will continue to diminish, violence will become less frequent, and economies will continue to grow steadily. More clinics and schools will be built, children will have access to smartphones, and we will see the best-educated generation emerge. Humanity will be better-connected and more integrated than ever before. Historians will look back at our generation and thank it for propelling humanity towards the most promising era in human history. And they will, of course, wonder why we didn't realize it was happening and adjust our policy approaches accordingly. This is especially pertinent for the West.

Why Hasn't the West Noticed?

Few leading Western minds are aware of – or if they are aware, they are not focused on – this explosive improvement in the human condition over the past three decades. The West needs to engage in deep self-reflection. In so doing, the West will see more clearly how and why it needs to change course if it is going to keep itself safe and prosperous in the twenty-first century. As George Orwell wrote, 'To see what is in front of one's nose needs a constant struggle.'

Honest self-reflection is never easy. As an amateur student of psychology, I learned from a very young age how prevalent self-deception can be. To break through the natural tendency to deceive ourselves, we have to deal with painful and uncomfortable truths. For example, few in the West will openly acknowledge that one key word explains why the West lost its way at the end of the Cold War: hubris.

As the spirits of Western leaders soared at their great victory over the Soviet Union, they switched off all the signals that could have alerted them to other big changes. This is, after all, a normal human response to a great victory. Fukuyama's essay 'The End of History?'

did a lot of brain damage to the West. It provided the opium to justify a complacent autopilot strategy at the precise moment when the West should have switched on its competitive engines. To clarify this point, let me put across a brief post-World War II version of history that no major Western historian has put across.

After the Second World War, the West remained focused and competitive. Western Europe worked hard to revive economies devastated by the years of war. America woke up and focused intensively on the new Soviet challenge. Both North America and Western Europe enjoyed healthy economic growth rates in the 1950s and 1960s. America's GDP grew at an average rate of 4.28 per cent, while Europe's grew even faster, at 4.87 per cent.[44] Even so, the United States was shocked when the Soviet Union became the first country to send a man into outer space. The United States ramped up its R&D investments to become the first country to land a man on the moon in 1969.

Through the 1970s and 1980s, as the Soviet threat gained pace, with Soviet-supported invasions in Cambodia and Afghanistan, the West remained alert. However, some seeds of complacency were taking root. After the massive decolonization of Asia, Africa and Latin America in the middle of the twentieth century, there were some concerns that these newly independent countries would challenge the West. Indeed, there were strong and vibrant Third World leaders – including

Jawaharlal Nehru of India, Gamal Abdel Nasser of Egypt, Sukarno of Indonesia and Norodom Sihanouk of Cambodia. Yet, as these two decades progressed, it became clear that, with the exception of the 'Four Tigers', most Third World economies were failing. The idea that any of these economies, including China and India, could challenge the West was laughable in Western eyes. As the Singapore Ambassador to the UN in the 1980s, I experienced the Western smugness over its inherent economic superiority. Western diplomats dispensed advice with thinly disguised condescension to the 88 per cent of the global population outside the West.

When the Soviet Union collapsed in 1991, it provided a massive boost to the sense of superiority that the West had begun to develop in the previous two decades (building on its highly developed sense of superiority over the past two centuries). This is why both American and European intellectuals believed that, having won the Cold War, the West could afford to relax and enjoy its good fortune. Western civilization had reached the final peak of human achievement. Other civilizations would have to struggle and work hard; the West need not. Willy Claes, the former Foreign Minister of Belgium, said in the early 1990s that: 'The Cold War has ended. There are only two superpowers left: the United States and Europe.'[45]

Western Hubris

This precise moment of maximum Western hubris coincided with the engines revving up in the rest of the world, particularly in China and India. China got going first, with Deng Xiaoping's breathtaking launch of the Four Modernizations in 1978. But Tiananmen in 1989 reinforced Western blindness. It strengthened Western governments' conviction that only their societies had found the magical formula for economic growth and political stability. Similarly, when senior Indian figures like Manmohan Singh and Montek Singh Ahluwalia went with their begging bowls to the IMF in 1990–91 to seek Western assistance in resolving a major financial crunch in India, the West's dominance seemed obvious.

Another event around the same time that prevented the West from changing course was the Asian Financial Crisis of 1997–8. In the mid-1990s, some in the West began to notice that a major Asian economic resurgence was happening. The desire to engage with Asia grew. I experienced this at first hand when I visited several European capitals to promote Singapore's idea of having the first Asia-Europe (ASEM) Leaders

Meeting. The first ASEM Summit was held in Bangkok with great fanfare on 1–2 March 1996. However, a year later, as soon as a string of Asian economies – including Indonesia, Malaysia, Thailand and South Korea – suffered in the Asian Financial Crisis, Europe once again lost interest in Asia. Western condescension returned with a vengeance.

In short, the two critical decades that saw the return of China and India, the 1990s and the 2000s, coincided with a period of maximum insularity and self-congratulation. Western leaders didn't notice – or ignored – some significant milestones. In 2014, measuring GDP in purchasing power parity terms (PPP), India surpassed Japan to become the world's third largest economy. China made even more impressive strides. In 2000, US GDP in nominal terms was nine times that of China. Owing to China's rapid growth in the ensuing decade, by 2010, US GDP was just 2.5 times that of China.[46] But in PPP terms, China emerged as the world's largest economy in 2014, even though it had been 10 per cent the size of the American economy in 1980.[47]

Strategic Errors: Islam, Russia and Meddling in World Affairs

If the West had noticed this great renaissance, they would have concentrated on the real issues shaking up their societies. Instead, blinded by hubris, the West made a series of strategic errors: intervening in Islamic countries, underestimating Islam as a religion and failing to address the root of the problem when it comes to terrorism. The most unwise intervention was to invade Iraq in March 2003. In theory, Iraq happened because of 9/11. In practice, it was just a demonstration of Western, especially American, hubris and strategic incompetence. To say that this war was a massive act of stupidity is an understatement. It was an act of folly on several counts. The United States invaded Iraq in revenge against the attack by an Islamic militant, Osama bin Laden. Yet in doing so, it removed a strong secular leader who was opposed to Osama bin Laden: Saddam Hussein. The United States also declared that it was worried about Iranian power. By destroying Saddam and the Taliban, America gave Iranian power a major boost. George W. Bush said that the invasion of Iraq was meant to create a strong, stable democracy in Iraq. Instead, with the assistance of the graduates of the leading universities of the world, he created a royal mess. Iraq has now become a textbook example of how not to invade a country. Singapore's founding Prime Minister, Lee Kuan Yew, a friend of the United States, noted wryly that even the Japanese had done better in the Second World War.

Iraq was a disaster. What made it worse was that it reinforced the conviction among 1.5 billion Muslims that the loss of Muslim lives did not matter to the West. A fair question that future historians may well address is whether the surge of Islamic terrorist incidents in Western capitals was an indirect consequence of this thoughtless campaign of bombing Islamic societies.

The West makes one fundamental mistake in all its dealings with the Islamic world: it underestimates the religion of Islam. Western analysts survey the Islamic world and see a string of weak societies. They associate the Islamic world with failed states, like Afghanistan and Somalia, or broken states, like Iraq and Syria. Yet even though many Islamic societies are struggling, Islam itself is only growing in strength. Indeed, to put it bluntly, Islam may well be the most dynamic and vibrant religion on Earth. According to Pew Research Center,

[The Muslim population] will grow more than twice as fast as the overall world population between 2015 and 2060 and, in the second half of this century, will likely surpass Christians as the world's largest religious group. While the world's population is projected to grow 32 per cent in the coming decades, the number of Muslims is expected to increase by 70 per cent – from 1.8 billion in 2015 to nearly 3 billion in 2060. In 2015, Muslims made up 24.1 per cent of the global population. Forty-five years later, they are expected to make up more than three-in-ten of the world's people (31.1 per cent).[48]

Islam is not just getting more adherents. Muslims are also becoming more religious. Since the Western mind likes to extrapolate Western assumptions into the human condition, it assumes that the modernization and economic development of any society will lead to less religiosity and more secularism. In the Islamic world, the reverse is happening: economic development and education are leading to greater religiosity. Greater numbers of women are wearing the hijab, even in parts of the world where it was rarely worn for centuries, including Central Asia and Southeast Asia. And, as the Islamic world becomes better educated and more religious, it remembers well the millennia of dealing with stronger and militarily superior Western societies. Many young Muslims resent the weakness of Islamic societies *vis-à-vis* the West. Many of them are therefore seduced by the violent rhetoric of Islamic clerics who point out the indifference of the West to the loss of Muslim lives. The young men who carried out terrorist attacks on 3 June 2017 in London were influenced by the Islamist preacher Musa Jibril, who tweeted: 'No intervention in Syria for over 2 years b/c those being killed are Muslim! Yet France quickly intervenes to massacre the Mali Muslims!'[49]

Let me put across a very sensitive point as delicately as possible. In going after a series of individuals who have been inflamed by such Islamist rhetoric, the West is pursuing a strategy as futile as that of cutting off the tip of the iceberg to save the *Titanic*. Until the iceberg is dealt with, the problem will never be solved. The West should engage in deep reflection on what it has done to the Islamic world for the past two centuries. This historical record will continue to haunt relations between Islam and the West over the next two centuries.

The West's second major strategic error was to further humiliate the already humiliated Russia. Gorbachev's unilateral dissolution of the Soviet empire was an unimaginable geopolitical gift to the West, especially America. The Russia that remained was a small shell of the Soviet empire. After winning the Cold War without firing a shot, it would have been wise for the West to heed Churchill's advice: 'In victory, magnanimity.' Instead, the West did the exact opposite. Contrary to the implicit assurances given to Gorbachev and Soviet leaders in 1990,[50] the West expanded NATO into previous Warsaw Pact countries, including the Czech Republic, Hungary, Poland, Bulgaria, Estonia, Latvia, Lithuania, Romania and Slovakia. Tom Friedman was dead right when he said, 'I opposed expanding NATO toward Russia after the Cold War, when Russia was at its most democratic and least threatening. It remains one of the dumbest things we've ever done and, of course, laid the ground-work for Putin's rise.'[51] The humiliation of Russia led to an inevitable blowback. The Russian people elected a strongman ruler, Vladimir Putin, to defend Russian national interests strongly.

Putin was elected President in 2000 and re-elected in 2012, and he also served as Prime Minister from 1999 to 2000 and 2008 to 2012. Yet, even while Putin was in office in the 2000s, the West threatened to expand NATO into Ukraine, despite the fact that eminent American statesmen like Henry Kissinger and Zbig-niew Brzezinski cautioned against it. Speaking of Ukraine, Kissinger said, '. . . I don't think it's a law of nature that every state must have the right to be an ally in the framework of NATO.'[52] Brzezinski said, 'Russia should be assured credibly that Ukraine will not become a member of NATO.'[53] These warnings were ignored. America supported the demonstrations against Presi-dent Viktor Yanukovych of Ukraine when his regime collapsed in 2014. Putin knew that the next Ukrainian government might push Ukraine into NATO. The result would have been that Crimea, which had been part of Russia from 1783 to 1954, would have been used by NATO against Russia. Putin felt that he simply had no choice but to take back Crimea. Even Gorbachev supported him.[54]

The Crimea episode showed that there is only so much humiliation that any nation can take. It was inevitable that the Russian people would say: enough is enough. Putin's election reflected the will of the people. They wanted a strongman ruler who could also poke the eyes of the West. He did this by invading Crimea and supporting Assad in Syria. There are no saints in geopolitical games. There is only tit for tat. If the West had shown respect for Russia instead of humiliating it, Putin would not have happened. In the summer of 2017, Putin was vilified by the American media for having interfered in American elections. Such interference is clearly wrong. Yet no American leader asked the obvious question in this 2017 debate: has America interfered in other countries' elections? Dov Levin of the Institute of Politics and Strategy at Carnegie Mellon University has compiled a database documenting that it has – more than 80 times between 1946 and 2000.[55] The West is no saint either, though it is regularly in danger of believing itself to be so.

And so to the West's third error: thoughtless intervention in the internal affairs of several countries. It is not a coincidence that the end of the Cold War saw a flurry of so-called 'colour' revolutions. A partial list includes the following: Yugoslavia in 2000 (Bulldozer), Georgia in 2003 (Rose), Ukraine in 2005 (Orange), Iraq in 2005 (Purple), Kyrgyzstan in 2005 (Tulip), Tunisia in 2010 (Jasmine), Egypt in 2011 (Lotus). Many of these colour revolutions were internally generated. However, when they surfaced, the West rushed to support them because in the minds of Western policy-makers, especially American ones, the export of democracy was an inherent good. Hence, they believed that they were living up to the highest moral standards of Western civilization.

Few in the Rest are convinced that the West's post-Cold War encouragement of democracy abroad represents a moral impulse. Instead, they see this as a last futile attempt to continue the two-century period of Western domination of world history through other means. They also notice the cynical promotion of democracy in adversarial countries like Iraq and Syria and not in friendly countries like Saudi Arabia. Most disastrously, when the intervention turns sour, as in Iraq or in Libya, the West walks away and takes on no moral responsibility for the adverse consequences. One painful truth that cannot be denied is that this thoughtless attempt to 'export democracy' has increased, not decreased, human suffering in many countries.

The West has lost its way significantly in the past three decades. It needs to change course. But before formulating a new strategy, the West needs to accept the changed mind-sets of non-Western populations. A resurgent Rest will not wear the same degree of

Western intervention as it did in the past. Until the West understands this, it will not understand why it needs a new strategy to remain successful.

One recent major event illustrates how ignorance of history causes misunderstandings between the West and the Rest. When 9/11 happened, most Americans felt they were innocent victims subject to an unprovoked attack. Most thoughtful international observers saw it as an inevitable blowback against the West's trampling on the Islamic world for several centuries. It was not just Muslims who believed that. One of Latin America's best novelists, Gabriel García Márquez, asked Americans:

> How does it feel now that horror is erupting in your own yard and not in your neighbor's living room? . . . Do you know that between 1824 and 1994 your country carried out 73 invasions in countries of Latin America? . . . For almost a century, your country has been at war with the entire world . . . How does it feel, Yank, knowing that on September 11th the long war finally reached your home?[56]

The West must recognize that all of humanity is one. Seven billion people live in 193 separate cabins on the same boat. The big problem is that while we have captains and crews taking care of each cabin, we have no captain or crew taking care of the whole boat. We can and should strengthen multilateral institutions of global governance, like the UN, the IMF, the World Bank and the WHO to take care of common global challenges.[57]

It is unhelpful that America is led by a President who refuses to recognize that we belong to a single human tribe living together on a fragile little planet, the only habitable place within the universe that we know of. If we screw up the only planet we have, we don't have a planet B to go to. Fortunately, the spread of modern reasoning by the West has made the rest of the world more rational and responsible.

Hence, even though Donald Trump, the leader of the best-educated society on Earth, is today making unwise decisions on climate change and triggering a new nuclear arms race, his kind of ignorance will eventually be overwhelmed by the broader, well-informed human community, which will rebel against such erroneous thinking. The West did the world a favour by sharing its culture of reasoning with the Rest. Now the Rest, after gaining the same access to the best sources of information, will be able to educate the West on the virtues of working together to protect and preserve planet Earth. Just as Donald Trump has pulled America backwards in the battle against climate change, the two most populous nations, China and India, have moved forward instead of blaming the West for creating the climate crisis (which is technically correct). And guess what? The Chinese and Indian people are supporting their governments. With greater access to information, they know that China and India will suffer if climate change worsens. There was no guarantee that China and India would continue to be reasonable on climate change after Trump made America unreasonable. The fact that they are is a clear cause for celebration.

A New Strategy: Minimalist, Multilateral and Machiavellian

Against this backdrop of a better-educated and more rational global community that will no longer wear Western meddling and condescension, the time has come for the West to abandon many of its short-sighted and self-destructive policies and pursue a completely new strategy towards the rest of the world. This new grand strategy can be described as the 3M strategy. The three Ms refer to Minimalist, Multilateral and Machiavellian.

The Minimalist approach is a critical first step. Many in the West believe that the West is an inherently benign force that is constantly trying to improve the world. Hence, they will be puzzled by this call to do less rather than more.

To understand why less will be better, the West needs to achieve a new consensus on its role in world history. When the West was overwhelmingly stronger than the rest of the world in the nineteenth and twentieth centuries, it had an explosive impact across the globe. Western boots trampled everywhere. The Rest had no choice but to bend to Western power. Now, as

Western power recedes, it is perfectly natural for the Rest to ask for new terms of engagement. Many parts of the world, especially Asia and Africa, would welcome a more restrained Western role.

Take the Islamic world, for example. They feel that the West has become trigger-happy since the end of the Cold War, and they resent it. Even worse, most of the countries recently bombed by the West have been Muslim countries, including Afghanistan, Iraq, Libya, Pakistan, Somalia, Sudan, Syria and Yemen. This is why many of the 1.5 billion Muslims believe that Muslim lives don't matter to the West.

As indicated earlier, the West needs to pose to itself a delicate and potentially explosive question: is there any correlation between the rise of Western bombing of Islamic societies and the rise of terrorist incidents in the West? It would be foolish to suggest an answer from both extremes: that there is an absolute correlation or zero correlation. The truth is probably somewhere in the middle. If so, isn't it wiser for the West to reduce its entanglements in the Islamic world?

Some of these entanglements have been very unwise. During the Cold War, the CIA instigated the creation of Al-Qaeda to fight the Soviet occupation of Afghanistan. The same organization bit the hand that fed it by attacking the World Trade Center on 11 September 2001. Sadly, America didn't learn the lesson from this mistake. In an effort to remove Assad in Syria, the

Obama administration transported ISIS fighters from Afghanistan to Syria to fight Assad.[58] To ensure that the ISIS fighters had enough funding, America didn't bomb the oil exports from ISIS-controlled zones in Syria to Turkey. Through all this, America declared that it was opposed to ISIS. In fact, some American agencies were supporting them, directly or indirectly.[59]

It is truly difficult to understand why America, a distant country protected by two oceans, decided to intertwine its destiny with the Islamic world. It may have made some strategic sense in the Cold War to prevent Soviet domination of the Middle East. Post-Cold War, especially with America becoming self-sufficient in energy, it makes no strategic sense. America should withdraw from its military engagements in the Middle East. Henceforth, there should be zero American bombs dropped in Islamic countries (though there is, perhaps, a case to argue in Afghanistan, because of the danger of the Taliban returning). Instead, America should enhance its diplomatic engagement and work with Europe to find geopolitically wise diplomatic solutions.

Will the Middle East become a darker place if America disengages militarily? Most American strategic thinkers are sure it would. Yet they also believed that the non-communist states in Southeast Asia would collapse like dominoes after the American forces withdrew ignominiously from Vietnam in 1975. The region appeared doomed to them then. Many British observers had long described Southeast Asia as 'the Balkans of Asia', because it is the most diverse corner of Asia, even more diverse than the actual Balkans.[60] No international observers expected Southeast Asia to become an oasis of peace and prosperity. But ASEAN kept progressing as the West kept retreating from the region.[61] More amazingly, while the West tried and failed to manage the transition away from absolute military rule in Syria, ASEAN did the same successfully in Myanmar. The thousand ASEAN meetings that the Myanmar military officials attended in neighbouring ASEAN capitals made them aware of how backward their country had become. So Myanmar switched course peacefully, without Western military intervention. The Rohingya killings and exodus were a tragedy, but they also reflected a last-ditch effort by the Myanmar military to embarrass Aung San Suu Kyi, both domestically and internationally.[62]

The Rest does not need to be saved by the West, educated by it on governmental structures, or shown the moral high ground. It most certainly does not need to be bombed. Stepping back will improve relations with many parts of the world – not only the Islamic world, but also China and Africa, which chafe under Western haughtiness. The Rest will continue to learn from the West in many areas. The EU's greatest achievement is that there is zero prospect of war between any two EU member states. ASEAN is trying to replicate this EU gold standard. The Nordic countries continue to excel in providing a good balance between economic growth and social harmony. This Nordic model will gradually become universalized. The United States continues to excel in higher education and entrepreneurship. The world will copy American best practices. Chinese university presidents regularly visit American campuses to learn from them. A minimalist global strategy by the West would promote even greater learning. It is always easier to learn from someone who doesn't exude an attitude of superiority.

The West also needs to understand the Rest better. This is where the second leg of the new strategy swings in: the Multilateral leg. Some leading Western minds accept the fact that the world has shrunk inexorably. We are reminded of this every year as each new crisis requires coordinated global actions. From the financial crisis (2008–9) to the Ebola outbreak (2014–16), from the Climate Change Summit in Paris (2015) to the terrorist attacks in leading capitals (2017), we learn that all cabins on the global boat must work together.

To work together, we need stronger and more effective global councils. Fortunately, as the eminent British historian Paul Kennedy has reminded us in his book *The Parliament of Man*, we do have a global parliament. It is the United Nations General Assembly (UNGA). Few Americans know that this is primarily an American creation; it was forged by President Truman in

1945. Truman was inspired by the following two lines from Tennyson's famous poem *Locksley Hall*:

Till the war-drum throbb'd no longer, and the battle-flags
   were furl'd
In the Parliament of man, the Federation of the world.[63]

Having served as Ambassador to the UN twice (from 1984 to 1989 and from 1998 to 2004), I know first-hand how debates in the UNGA can provide a good flavour of the thinking of 7.3 billion people. When ambassadors to the UN speak, they would be excoriated by their populations if they didn't express the points of view of their people. As a result, a real cacophony of voices is heard.

Since many criticisms of the West are expressed in the UNGA, the West, especially America, has tried to both marginalize and ignore UN debates. Daniel Patrick Moynihan, US Ambassador to the UN in the 1970s, wrote in his memoirs: 'The Department of State desired that the United Nations prove utterly ineffective in whatever measures it undertook. This task was given to me, and I carried it forward with no inconsiderable success.'[64] The American political scientist Edward Luck has said: 'The last thing the US wants is an independent UN throwing its weight around . . . [The US isn't] going to allow the organization to dictate things inconsistent with the objectives of US leadership.'[65]

America marginalizes the world's voices. Here again, let me ask a politically sensitive question: would there have been fewer terrorist attacks on Western capitals had they paid more heed to the voices of the Rest? Why did the first Iraq invasion by father President Bush in 1991 succeed spectacularly, while the second Iraq invasion by son President Bush in 2003 failed miserably? The most essential difference is that the elder Bush sought and obtained the support of the UN. Virtually the whole world, including China and Russia, supported this invasion. By contrast, his son went against the consensus of the UN. Virtually the whole world, including China and Russia, opposed the invasion.

There is an obvious lesson to be learned from these two Iraq wars, yet few American intellectuals dare to admit publicly they were wrong in supporting the second Iraq War. Someone should start a 'mea culpa' movement in America. Each leading American intellectual who supported the war in 2003 should publish an essay on why he or she failed to listen to the overwhelming sentiments of the rest of the world. In so doing, they will expose some of the strong self-deception that has characterized American foreign-policy thinking over the past fifteen years.

One myth that surprisingly many Americans believe is that America is often prevented from doing the right thing in the UN (for example, in Syria) because of the opposition of non-democratic states like Russia and

China. The remarkably sanctimonious statements made by the American Ambassadors to the UN Samantha Power and Nikki Haley reinforce this belief. Nikki Haley said, after Russia and China blocked sanctions on Syria in February 2017, 'They put their friends in the Assad regime ahead of our global security . . . They turned away from defenceless men, women and children who died gasping for breath when Assad's forces dropped their poisonous gas.'[66] But American intervention in Syria is also opposed by the world's largest democracy, India, and the world's third-largest democracy, Indonesia. Why is America not listening to its fellow democracies? Or do the opinions of non-Western democracies not matter? This is what a leading Indian official, Shyam Saran, wrote about Western intervention:

> In most cases, the post-intervention situation has been rendered much worse, the violence more lethal, and the suffering of the people who were supposed to be protected much more severe than before. Iraq is an earlier instance; Libya and Syria are the more recent ones. A similar story is playing itself out in Ukraine. In each case, no careful thought was given to the possible consequences of the intervention.[67]

He also wrote, '[Europe] has added to instability and disruption in West Asia with its ill-considered interventions in Libya and Syria.'[68]

This is why multilateral institutions and processes matter. They provide the best platform for hearing and understanding the views of the world. The next time the West wants to get on its moral high horse and intervene in another non-Western country it should first convene a meeting of the UN General Assembly. This is the only forum where all 193 sovereign countries can speak freely. And it is where the West will get a good understanding of what 88 per cent of the world's population thinks.

Over the past thirty years, as Western power has waned, instead of listening to the majority opinions of humanity the West has regularly tried to justify its ignoring of majority worldviews by attacking the UN. There has been a dedicated American campaign – supported by European cowardice – to delegitimize the UN, especially the UNGA.[69] Yet, as Margaret Thatcher shrewdly observed, 'The United Nations is only a mirror held up to our own uneven, untidy and divided world. If we do not like what we see there's no point in cursing the mirror, we had better start by reforming ourselves.'[70] We need to build a new global consensus. The beautifully written Charter of the United Nations and the Universal Declaration of Human Rights, which espouse many noble universal values, can provide the foundation for the values of this new consensus.

The re-legitimization of the UN is therefore another simple step away from the current flawed and arrogant

Western strategies. There is no better opportunity to do this than now. In a somewhat miraculous move, the UN elected António Guterres as UN Secretary-General in 2016. It was a miracle because he is shrewd and experienced. Even better, he is European and comes from a NATO state – Portugal. If the West cannot work with a staunchly pro-Western Secretary-General like him to revive and strengthen the UN, who can it work with?

Yet, altruism never works in international affairs. The West will only change course and work to strengthen, not undermine, multilateral institutions when it concludes after hard-headed analysis that it is in its long-term interests to do so. This is why the third prong of a new Western strategy has to be based on a Machiavellian approach. What approach will best serve the long-term global interests of the West?

Machiavelli is both one of the best-known and least understood Western figures. In the popular imagination he is seen as a personification of evil. Yet, most serious philosophers regard him as one of the wisest thinkers of all times. The great philosopher Isaiah Berlin reminded us in his classic essay that Machiavelli's key goal was to promote *virtù* ('virtue'). His goal was to generate a better society that would enhance the well-being of its citizens.[71]

In our rapidly changing world, the West needs to learn more from Machiavelli and deploy more strategic cunning to protect its long-term interests. Strategic cunning is as old as the hills. Two thousand five hundred years ago, the legendary Chinese strategist Sun Tzu advised, 'Know thy self, know thy enemy. A thousand battles, a thousand victories.' The most difficult part of this piece of advice is 'Know thy self'. Few in the West are aware of how quickly the Western share of global power has shrunk, as documented in the opening charts.

A general going into a battlefield with an army twice the size of his opponent's will adopt one strategy. However, if his army shrinks to half the size of his opponent's and he maintains the same strategy, he is committing a strategic folly. This is what the West is doing. Its global power is rapidly shrinking, but it proceeds on autopilot.

The West on Autopilot: Europe and America Do Not Face the Same Challenges

To put it bluntly, there may have been a time (perhaps at the end of the Cold War) when 12 per cent of the world's population could afford to impose demands on China (20 per cent of the world's population), anger the Islamic world (20 per cent of the world's population), ignore the demographic explosion in Africa (15 per cent of the world's population) and humiliate Russia (the world's second largest nuclear power). That time has gone. The West will have to learn to be as strategically cunning as Mao Zedong (a good student of Sun Tzu). Mao succeeded in battle after battle against the Kuomintang and the invading Japanese by fighting with the primary enemy and setting aside the struggle against the secondary enemy. It was brilliant of him to invite Nixon to visit Beijing when his primary concern was a war with the Soviet Union.

The reality that the West has to deal with is that the primary strategic challenge for America is not the same as the primary strategic challenge for Europe. For America, it is China. For Europe, it is the Islamic world at its doorstep. Facts are facts. Yet each year, when the best Western strategic thinkers converge at the Munich Security Conference in February, not one Western strategic thinker can state the most obvious and important thing: American and European interests have diverged. The election of Trump has brought this divergence out into the open. It may well go down as one of Trump's biggest contributions to world history. Chancellor Merkel said in May 2017, 'The times in which [Germany] could fully rely on others are partly over. I have experienced this in the last few days. We Europeans really have to take our destiny into our own hands.'[72]

Both America and Europe would be better off if they were to become more strategically cunning in defending their respective interests. For Europe, it is clear that the primary threat is not going to come from Russia. Unlike during the Cold War, no Russian tanks threaten Europe. Russia is now a secondary challenge. Hence, Europe should make peace with Putin. Nor is Europe threatened by Chinese Intercontinental Ballistic Missiles. Instead, China's economic development is good for Europe's interests. Why? Europe's primary threat is spillover instability from the Islamic world. As long as North Africa and the Middle East are populated with struggling states, migrants will come into Europe, stirring populist parties. However, if Europe helps North Africa to replicate the successful economic development stories of Malaysia (described earlier) and Indonesia, Europe will have built a strategic bulwark against unmanageable migrant flows. In short, it is in Europe's strategic interest to import the East Asian economic success stories into North Africa. Hence, Europe should work with China, not against China, to build up North Africa.

Fostering the economic development of North Africa is not an idle dream. The per capita incomes of Algeria and Tunisia were higher than those of Malaysia and Indonesia thirty years ago (see Figure 4), yet Malaysia and Indonesia have grown more rapidly in the past three decades. What Indonesia and Malaysia have accomplished today, Algeria and Tunisia can accomplish tomorrow. Young Algerians and Tunisians should be sent to East Asia to study. Europeans should feel a desperate sense of urgency in dealing with North Africa, because, behind North Africa, an even bigger demographic explosion is coming. Africa's population will become as large as Asia's by 2100. Then there will be 4.5 billion people in Africa. How will an ageing population of 450 million Europeans deal with this demographic explosion? Europe must become cunning and focus on its own existential challenge.

The Europeans also need better leadership. Trump and his advisers are right when they say that Europeans have been free-riding on America by not paying their fair share for NATO. What they don't add is that Americans have taken advantage of this European strategic

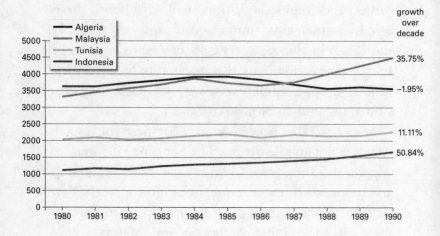

Figure 4. GDP per capita, 1980–90[73]

passivity to hijack European states and get them to support various American initiatives that are against long-term European interests. Geopolitics is, at the end of the day, about geography. The Americans have destabilized Europe's geographical neighbourhood.

The Europeans have not been cunning enough in protecting their own strategic interests in the Middle East and Russia. The Americans can walk away from the disastrous consequences of destabilizing Ukraine; the Europeans cannot. The Europeans were technically right in saying that Russians violated international law in Ukraine. Yet, as Ambassador Puri – the representative of the world's largest democracy, India – has said, 'It can be argued that given the impunity with which international law and state sovereignty were being violated all around, the Russian step was merely one – which the West now protests against the most – in a long list, including Iraq, Kosovo, Libya, Syria and Yemen.'[74]

Most countries in the world are bewildered by the American insistence on humiliating Russia. They are even more bewildered by European complicity. Trump and his team were initially showing strategic common sense by not antagonizing Putin, yet few European leaders have shown their support for this common sense, confirming once again the lack of strategic cunning in Europe. Senator McCain is right to rail against alleged Russian meddling in American elections. Western logic teaches us that McCain's complaint implies a universal moral rule: no country should interfere in any other country's elections. Would McCain agree to a similar rule for America not interfering in any other country's elections? And if America exhibits double standards in such behaviour, would Europe point that out?

America is an ocean away. It can and should walk away from its multiple engagements in the Islamic world to focus on its primary challenge: China. Future historians will wonder why America showered geopolitical gifts upon China as it was rising. In the early 2000s, in the most rapid phase of China's development, America decided to invade Iraq and get mired in a swamp. And how did this strategic folly come about? It happened because America reacted emotionally, instead of rationally, to 9/11.

The Islamic world is not America's primary strategic challenge. It is a secondary challenge. Hence, it should make peace with the Islamic world, not rile it. With the shale revolution, America doesn't even need oil from the Gulf. Paradoxically, its naval fleet in the Gulf protects oil supplies to China, as China depends greatly on oil imports from the Gulf region. America has also demonstrated strategic stupidity in dealing with Iran. It has allowed the painful memories of the 1979 occupation of the American embassy in Tehran (which is now almost forty years ago) to trump cunning strategic calculations. Iran will never be a threat to America. Instead, it could enhance America's strategic options. One of Obama's biggest gifts to America was the nuclear deal with Iran. Trump should build on it by establishing diplomatic relations. The best way to transform Iranian society is to send thousands, if not millions, of American tourists to the country. In 2012, Christopher Thornton wrote in *The Atlantic* that 'a 2009 World Public Opinion poll found that 51 per cent of Iranians hold a favourable opinion of Americans, a number consistent with other polls, meaning that Americans are more widely liked in Iran than anywhere else in the Middle East.'[75] Shrewd American geopolitical policies should take advantage of this. Instead, foolishly, Trump is trying to derail this Iran agreement. The US Congress unwisely imposed new sanctions on Iran in 2017.

The big danger that America faces if it wakes up and begins to deal with China is that it will make the same mistakes that the Soviet Union made when it dealt with the US. The Soviet Union saw America as a military competitor. In fact, America was its economic competitor, and it was the collapse of the Soviet economy that led to America's victory. Similarly, for America, China is an economic competitor, not a military competitor. The biggest mistake that America could make is to step up its military deployments in East Asia to balance a resurgent China. The more that America spends on military expenses, the less effective it will be in the long run in dealing with a far stronger and bigger Chinese economy. In 2015, America spent 3.3 per cent of its GDP on defence; China spent only 1.9 per cent.

This American tendency to outspend the rest of the world also has other negative consequences. The old adage says that if you only have a hammer, every problem looks like a nail. Consequently, American strategic behaviour has been distorted. Brawn replaces brains. Strategic cunning is rarely deployed in American responses to global crises.

In 2017, Trump experienced his first series of crises with North Korea. Kim Jong Un carried out tests and fired missiles. America reacted in a Pavlovian fashion. It sent a naval fleet led by USS *Carl Vinson* to be parked near North Korea. Rex Tillerson announced that the era of 'strategic patience' was over. Did these military responses work? Did they change North Korean behaviour? No.

Kim Jong Un knew better than anyone that America didn't have a military option. A military strike against North Korea (*à la* Syria) would have led to an artillery barrage against Seoul. A million people could have died, and the resulting war would not have been between North Korea and America; in a replay of 1950, China would have got involved.

There were other options America could have deployed. There is one major historical fact that most American policy-makers do not seem to know. Diplomatic immunity was invented over 2,000 years ago to enable diplomatic envoys to visit enemy capitals without getting their heads chopped off by angry kings and queens. Hence, if North Korea is an enemy, the logical response is to establish diplomatic relations with Pyongyang. However, since Washington DC is often shrouded in political correctness, it is the only capital that believes that establishment of diplomatic relations is an act of approval. Actually, it is supposed to signal a lack of trust among nations. As a consequence, America under-uses its diplomatic opportunities.

If it were to utilize diplomatic tools, it would first create a strategic alignment of interests between China and America on the Korean peninsula. How would this be done? Professor Robert MacFarquhar has advised that America could provide China with a strong assurance that a reunified Korean peninsula would be a neutral country (like Austria after the Second World War). All American troops and bases would leave a reunified Korea. And would this be a strategic defeat for America? Or would this be a cunning move by America to create a fiercely independent country on China's doorstep? Just as history and geography made Vietnam fiercely independent of China after American troops left, the same would happen to Korea. In short, strategic cunning can be more effective than military brawn in solving complex geopolitical challenges.

Sadly, this reliance on military brawn is not confined to the right wing in America. The left-wing liberals also feel a need to demonstrate their hawkish credentials. Hillary Clinton demonstrated this as Secretary of State in advocating the bombing of Syria. Even Obama felt a need to step up the bombings of Afghanistan and Pakistan with unmanned drones. Quite remarkably, the only time when the liberal intelligentsia praised Donald Trump was when he bombed Syria after an ostensible chemical attack by President Assad on 6 April 2017. America needs to engage in deep reflection on why American strategic behaviour relies more on bombs than brains. Ironically, China may be privately happy that America focuses on military solutions while it focuses on economic development.

In theory, China will win in economic competition, because it has a much larger population: 1.37 billion, as opposed to America's 321 million. Yet, America has outperformed every other economy in the world by being able to attract the best and brightest of the 7 billion people on Earth. This is why many of America's greatest universities, schools and companies are led by American citizens born overseas. The H1B visa, which allows US companies to employ foreign nationals in certain occupations, is part of America's strategic answer to China's population advantage. Yet it is precisely at the moment when America needs more H1B visas to deal with China's economic competition that America is reducing the number of H1B visas.

All this is a result of the lack of long-term strategic cunning. This is why the Machiavellian dimension is so critical if the West is to successfully adjust and adapt to its new position in the world.

A More Dangerous World

My Asian, African and Latin American friends will be troubled by my call to the West to be cunning: they will fear that that I am trying to prolong Western domination of our global order. That's not my reason for calling for more strategic cunning. I am doing so because a naïve and ideological West is dangerous. The failure of the West to make major strategic adjustments is responsible for many of the mishaps the world has experienced recently. The world will become more unstable unless the West radically changes course.

Democracies are not designed to take on long-term challenges. They can respond to immediate threats, like Hitler or Stalin. However, even if the threat is going to be faced by the grandchildren of the voters, voters will not vote for a politician who says: 'Let's sacrifice now to save our grandchildren.'

Western thinkers are right to speak about the many virtues of democratic political systems. They are also right in saying that democracy is the worst form of government, except for the alternatives. It is also true that because of their many checks and balances, democracies have demonstrated long-term resilience.

However, the West is wrong in believing that democracy is a necessary condition for economic success. If it were, China could not and should not have succeeded. But it has. This is also why many in the West deeply resent China's success. It undermines many key pillars of Western ideology.

The shortcomings of democracy are dominating Western societies at a time when these societies have to make major strategic changes. And failures to make strategic changes at the right time do lead to disasters.

Many of the problems the West is encountering now are the result of the strategic misjudgements of yesterday. Chas Freeman, a distinguished former American ambassador, has made the same point:

> The risks the world now faces were not (and are not) inevitable. They are the product of lapses of statesmanship and failures to consider how others see and react to us. The setbacks to America's ability to shape the international environment to its advantage are not the result of declining capacity on its part. They are the consequence of a failure to adapt to new realities and shifting power balances.[76]

A few examples will drive home the point. In early 2017, Europe was startled by President Erdoğan's efforts to use Turkish populations in Europe to vote in favour of constitutional changes to entrench his power. All the blame was heaped on Erdoğan, one man. But how much of Turkish anger was a result of being insulted by Europe for decades? Turkey applied for EU membership in 1987 and never got in. Austria, Cyprus, Malta, Sweden, Finland, Hungary, Poland, Romania, Slovakia, Latvia, Estonia, Lithuania, Bulgaria, the Czech Republic, Slovenia and Croatia applied later and did. You don't insult a country and not face consequences. Even more stupidly, the Europeans kept Turkey out and allowed Turks in (who want to vote for Erdoğan). It would have been wiser to keep Turks out and admit Turkey into the EU (with restrictions on free movement of labour). The jobs generated inside Turkey would have kept Turks at home.

Similarly, it was a folly for Europe to launch the Common Agricultural Policy (CAP) in 1962. It enriched a few European farmers. It impoverished millions of African farmers, especially in North Africa. Why are millions of Africans trying to get into Europe illegally? Because Europe lost its strategic common sense. By not exporting jobs to Africa, it designed policies that would inevitably import Africans into Europe.

This is why the Rest should wish and hope for a more cunning and calculating West to manage the next thirty years. Here are some key economic forecasts about the world in 2050. In 1950, the American-European (UK, France and Germany) share of World GDP was 43 per cent.[77] By 2050, it will have shrunk to 24 per cent.[78] The population figures are even more stunning. As Swedish physician and epidemiologist Hans Rosling has documented, in 1950, Europe's share of the world's population was 22 per cent, while Africa's was 9 per cent. By 2050, Europe's share will have shrunk to 7 per cent, while Africa's will have exploded to 39 per cent. If Europe continues on autopilot, or sinks into despair or racially and religiously motivated ideological approaches to declining power in population shifts, this will be an act of collective suicide. It will also be hugely damaging for the Rest, as Europe and America flail around.

The explosive expansion of Western power into every nook and cranny of the world has done both good and evil (including the genocidal disappearance of many peoples), yet the 88 per cent of the world's population outside the West have absorbed a great deal of Western wisdom. They can and are forging ahead and building their own futures.

By a remarkable accident of history, the most distant Asian society from Europe – Japan – became the first non-Western society to modernize, through the Meiji Reformation in the 1860s. A century later, more Asian societies emulated Japan. All this has led to the great and unstoppable Asian resurgence. Now, through another accident of history, the virtues of modernization are poised to enter Arab, Turkish and Persian societies, because all these societies are genuinely amazed by the spectacular success of Asia, from China to India, and keen to replicate such success. It is not an accident that the custodian of the two holiest Islamic sites, King Salman of Saudi Arabia, decided to make a month-long trip to Asia, instead of Europe, in early 2017 as his first overseas tour. By looking East instead of West, these Islamic societies will slowly transform and modernize.

The West can accelerate a two-way street of learning between Western and Eastern Muslims by quietly terminating its two-century-long policy of interfering in Islamic societies. A good start, as indicated earlier, will be to stop all bombing of Islamic countries. After a few painful bumps in the road, the Arabs, Turks and Persians will reach various mutual adjustments. Europe's shining example of the culture of peace, which has been replicated in the more diverse Southeast Asia, will slowly seep into the Middle East too. This is the most significant advantage that will come from a strategic and cunning withdrawal of Western power from this region.

Few Western minds can conceive of a peaceful Middle East. Sam Huntington, one of America's most thoughtful analysts, famously declared that 'Islam has bloody borders.' 9/11 only accentuated the belief that Muslims are inherently violent. If this were true, I should live each day in extreme fear. Singapore is a small, predominantly Chinese state surrounded by two large, mostly Muslim states: Malaysia and Indonesia. Despite having had multiple problems with both of them over the decades, the chances of Singapore going to war with either state is practically zero today. Why? All three countries have learnt that wars don't make sense. We are focused on economic growth and working together to promote it. The sort of sensible decisions that Singapore, Malaysia and Indonesia have made are being replicated everywhere. A Middle East region with less Western meddling will ultimately be a predominantly peaceful region.

Similarly, the 1.3 billion people of India (who will become 1.66 billion by 2100[79]) will benefit from a graceful withdrawal of Western power. One of the manifest absurdities of our time is that the UK and France remain as 'permanent members' of the UN Security Council (UNSC), passing mandatory resolutions that the rest of the world has to comply with. They are only there because of their nineteenth-century prowess, not their twenty-first-century promise. Indeed, in 2045, on the 100th anniversary of the UNSC, if the UK and France remain permanent members and India is out, the UNSC would have lost all its credibility. No serious country would then comply with its resolutions.

As the Western share of the global population and of global power recedes, the West should calculate that it is in its best interests to have a stronger rules-based order. One way to do this is to strengthen, not weaken, the UNSC. The best way to strengthen the credibility of the UNSC is for the UK to give up its seat to India and, as I argued in *The Great Convergence*, for France to share its seat with the EU.[80] What I am advocating here is plain common sense for long-term European interests. Yet, it shows how far away the Europeans are from strategic cunning that the most obvious solutions for their long-term interests are neither conceivable nor mentionable in European discourse.

Western humility would be good for the 1.4 billion people in China, too. The biggest act of strategic folly that America could commit would be to make a futile attempt to derail China's successful development before China clearly emerges as number one in the world again. Barack Obama avoided this temptation from 2009 to 2016. Trump is unpredictable. It is truly dangerous that there is a significant group of thinkers, policy-makers and activists in Washington DC who are quietly plotting and planning various ways of derailing China. Such activity can only give credence to the hawkish voices in the country and result in the emergence of an angry nationalist China.[81]

Today, under Trump, America is focused on military competition. He has announced that he will increase the US naval fleet from 272 ships to 350.[82] This is strategic folly. A more cunning America would focus on reducing its navy, not expanding it. And would the world collapse? Would trade routes be threatened? And if trade routes suffer, would America suffer more or would the world's number one exporter, China, suffer more? In short, some strategic common sense would encourage America to be more prudent than expansionary in its military spending. It is an even bigger folly for Trump to announce a nuclear arms race, as nuclear weapons remain the only force that could destroy the world.

Instead of igniting an arms race with China, America should heed the cunning advice given by Bill Clinton when he spoke at Yale in 2003. This is what he said:

> If you believe that maintaining power and control and absolute freedom of movement and sovereignty is important to your country's future, there's nothing inconsistent in that [the US continuing to behaving unilaterally]. [The US is] the biggest, most powerful country in the world now. We've got the juice and we're going to use it . . . But if you believe that we should be trying to create a world with rules and partnerships and habits of behaviour that we would like to live in when we're no longer the military political economic superpower in the world, then you wouldn't do that. It just depends on what you believe.[83]

Bill Clinton was bravely advising his fellow Americans to begin preparing for a world where America is no longer number one. It was brave for him to do so, as it is almost taboo in America to speak of America becoming number two (although it will inevitably become number two). So what is the best outcome for America when it becomes number two? The best outcome would be a number one power (namely, China) that respects 'rules and partnerships and habits of behaviour' that America could live with.

And what would be the best way to slip on these 'handcuffs' of 'rules and partnerships and habits of behaviour' onto China? This is where Bill Clinton was being cunning. He was advising his fellow Americans to slip the handcuffs of 'rules and partnerships' onto themselves. Once America had created a certain pattern of behaviour for the world's number one power, the same pattern of behaviour would be inherited by the next number one power, namely China. The good news is that China, for its own reasons, is happy to live in a world dominated by multilateral rules and processes. Xi Jinping explained why in the two brilliant speeches he gave in Davos and Geneva in January 2017. Xi said, for example, in Geneva:

> Economic globalization, a surging historical trend, has greatly facilitated trade, investment, flow of people and technological advances . . . 1.1 billion people have been lifted out of poverty, 1.9 billion people now have access to safe drinking water, 3.5 billion people have gained access to the Internet, and the goal has been set to eradicate extreme poverty by 2030.[84]

However, what Xi did not say is that China, unlike America, does not have a messianic impulse to change the world. If order abroad facilitates order at home, China would be happy. Hence, by following Bill Clinton's cunning advice, America would be laying the foundation for a more orderly world.

A Better World – for Americans and Europeans

All these recommendations are based on a fundamental assumption that Western minds need to understand that, for over two centuries, they have been aggressive and interventionist. Now it is in their strategic interests to be prudent and non-interventionist. This will benefit the world, as outlined above. It will also benefit Western populations.

The West was the first civilization to break out of the clutches of superstition and ignorance that dominated the feudal eras of human history. The West also deserves the credit for carrying humanity to our current era of unprecedented peace and prosperity. Yet instead of celebrating these achievements, Western populations are pessimistic and despondent. According to the 2017 Deloitte Millennial Survey, 'Millennials in emerging markets generally expect to be both financially (71 per cent) and emotionally (62 per cent) better off than their parents. This is in stark contrast to mature markets, where only 36 per cent of millennials predict they will be financially better off than their parents and 31 per cent say they'll be happier.'[85] Similarly, according to the 2014 Pew Global Attitudes Survey,

'Most of those surveyed in richer nations think children in their country will be worse off financially than
their parents. In contrast, emerging and developing
nations are more optimistic that the next generation
will have a higher standard of living.'[86]

A less adversarial relationship between the West and
the Rest will help to dispel the clouds of pessimism that
now envelop Western societies. Erstwhile adversaries,
like China and the Islamic world, will be seen as strong
potential economic partners, not threats. When the
global middle-class population explodes from 1.8 billion in 2009 to 4.9 billion in 2030,[87] it will present new
opportunities for the competitive Western economies.

There is no doubt that the Western elites failed to
prepare their populations for the inevitable 'creative
destruction' that flowed from China's admission into
the WTO in 2001. As a result, the elites have lost the
trust of their populations. Martin Wolf described it
well: 'The elites – the policy-making, business and
financial elites – are increasingly disliked. You need to
make policy which brings people to think again that
their societies are run in a decent and civilized way.'[88]

Fortunately, this problem can be solved. Many societies, from Sweden to Singapore, have devised various
social safety nets to help the working classes handle the
disruptions of globalization. The solution is not to close
the doors to free trade. The theory of comparative
advantage still holds true. Asia is rising because it

remains committed to this theory. The Western elites need to regain their intellectual confidence and explain again to the masses how it works. To do so, however, they have to overcome their current bitter divisiveness.

Unfortunately, the current political environments in both America and Europe are not conducive to deep, long-term reflection. In theory, this reflection should come easily to the liberal and open-minded elites. However, on both sides of the Atlantic, they are now consumed by different kinds of civil wars.

America has never been as deeply divided as it has become since Trump's election. Trump is clearly ignorant about the world. His constant emphasis on 'America first' is alienating. However, the liberal opposition is not making matters any better. None of the liberal bastions of thought are prepared to contemplate the possibility that they, too, may have been part of the problem.

The *New York Times*, for example, remains unrepentant. It takes no responsibility for failing to explain why so many working-class – especially white – Americans had become so disconnected with the messianic worldview of American elites. The elites clearly enjoyed the rich pickings they got from surfing on the globalization that America launched. They refused to see the pain that the same massive change had wrought upon the masses. There is one glaring statistic to sum this up: 63 per cent of Americans don't have enough savings to cover a $500 emergency.[89] In short, while America is wasting trillions fighting unnecessary wars and deploying unnecessary aircraft carriers, 200 million Americans live on the edge. This defies common sense.

Trump was not wrong when he advocated the goal of 'America first'. This is what his people want. However, his methods of achieving this are totally flawed. If he cuts off America from global trade flows, he will deliver an 'America last'. What America needs is a strong degree of bipartisan consensus on how to engage the world intelligently so that all Americans, especially working-class Americans, are better off. Instead, at a time when the country should come together, it has never been more divided, and it is badly divided because both sides are being ideological. If both sides were to become more Machiavellian in their calculations, they would agree on some obvious and fundamental things that America needs to do. However, to reach any such agreement, they have to understand the Rest better.

Unfortunately, any such understanding is undermined by American insularity. Every fortnight, my home in Singapore receives, by mail, a copy of the *New York Review of Books* (*NYRB*). It is probably the best-written magazine in the world. It is such a joy to read. But every time I pick it up, I wince when I look at the table of contents. Almost all the writers are Western. There are 4.43 billion Asians out of a global population of 7.12 billion people, and the *NYRB* apparently can't find any Asian writers. Perhaps it cannot find ones who reinforce the Western *Weltanschauung* ('worldview'). One of Asia's best novelists is Amitav Ghosh. He told me that his relationship with the *New Yorker*, another great magazine, came to an end when he resisted their attempts to get his writing to fit into their traditional worldview.[90]

As long as liberal Americans believe that they have the most liberal minds in the world, they will never wake up and understand the closed mental universes they have boxed themselves into. Liberalism has created an attitude of intellectual superiority, especially towards the rest of the world. Most European intellectuals, who are more aware of their own troubled history and the damage that European colonization did to the world, do not share the messianic impulse of American intellectuals. Nonetheless, there is a similar reluctance to accept the new reality that Europe must also make structural adjustments to cope with a resurgent Rest.

So – Has the West Lost It?

The crux of the problem facing the West is that neither the conservatives nor the liberals, neither the right wing nor the left wing, understand that history changed direction at the beginning of the twenty-first century. The era of Western domination is coming to an end. They should lift their sights from their domestic civil wars and focus on the larger global challenges. Instead they are, in various ways, accelerating their irrelevance and disintegration.*

It is not inevitable that China will lead the world, even though it is inevitable that China will have the world's

---

* The European leaders, especially Merkel and Macron, were right to warn Trump in private that the American decision to withdraw from the Paris Agreement would increase the likelihood of a world led by China. According to the minutes from a May 2017 G7 meeting obtained by *Der Spiegel*, Angela Merkel told Trump, 'If the world's largest economic power were to pull out, the field would be left to the Chinese.' *Der Spiegel* reported that Merkel added that Xi Jinping is clever and would take advantage of the vacuum created. When it was clear that Trump would ignore wise European advice and make the US withdraw from the Agreement, Macron said resignedly, 'Now China leads.' [91]

largest economy. Nor is it inevitable that the past two centuries of Western domination of world history will be replaced by two centuries of Asian domination, even though it is inevitable that the Asian share of the global GDP will far surpass that of the West.

It *is* inevitable that the world will face a troubled future if the West can't shake its interventionist impulses, refuses to recognize its new position, or decides to become isolationist and protectionist.

This is why this book is intended, ultimately, as a gift to the West. It reminds the West how much it has done to elevate the human condition higher than ever before. And it would be a great tragedy if the West were to be the world's primary instigator of turbulence and uncertainty at the hour of humanity's greatest promise. If this were to happen, future historians will be puzzled that the most successful civilization in human history failed to exploit the greatest opportunity ever presented to humanity. A simple dose of Machiavelli is what we need to save the West and the Rest. Otherwise, the West really has lost it.

Notes

1 https://www.marxists.org/reference/archive/machia-velli/works/prince/ch25.htm

2 https://www.siemens.com/content/dam/internet/siemens-com/customer-magazine/2017/industry/february/other_assets/mckinsey-asia-and-the-new-infrastructure-opportunity.pdf

3 https://www.lrb.co.uk/2016/11/14/rw-johnson/trump-some-numbers

4 https://www.ft.com/content/1c7270d2-6ae4-11e7-b9c7-15af748b60d0

5 https://archive.org/stream/LeoStraussThoughtsOnMach iavelli_201411 [Leo_Strauss]_Thoughts_on_Machiavelli_djvu.txt

6 Isaiah Berlin, 'A Special Supplement: The Question of Machiavelli', *New York Review of Books*, 4 November 1971: http://www.nybooks.com/articles/1971/11/04/a-special-supplement-the-question-of-machiavelli/ (accessed 6 June 2017).

7 https://newrepublic.com/article/77728/history-violence

8 Steven Pinker, 'A History of Violence', *New Republic*, 19 March 2007: https://newrepublic.com/article/77728/history-violence/ (accessed 28 November 2017).

9 Max Roser, 'Proof that Life is Getting Better for Humanity, in 5 Charts', published online at https://www.vox.com/the-big-idea/2016/12/23/14062168/history-global-conditions-charts-life-span-poverty

10 Peter Diamandis, Twitter post, 11 November 2016: https://twitter.com/PeterDiamandis/status/797119982224097281/

11 Johan Norberg, 'Despite Many Obstacles, the World is Getting Better', *Guardian*, 14 February 2017: https://www.theguardian.com/global-development-professionals-network/2017/feb/14/despite-many-obstacles-the-world-is-getting-better

12 Bertrand Russell, 'The Study of Mathematics', *New Quarterly*, November 1907.

13 Elsje Fourie, 'Model Students: Policy Emulation, Modernization, and Kenya's *Vision 2030*', *African Affairs*, Vol. 113, Issue 453, 1 October 2014, pp. 540–62.

14 'FT interview: Meles Zenawi, Ethiopian prime minister', *Financial Times*, 6 February 2007: https://www.ft.com/content/4db917b4-b5bd-11db-9eea-0000779e2340 (accessed 10 August 2017).

15 'Ethiopia's Renaissance Follows Korean Development', *Korea Herald*, 26 April 2015: http://www.koreaherald.com/view.php?ud=20150426000317 (accessed 10 August 2017).

16 Anthony Elson, 'The Economic Growth of East Asia and Latin America in Comparative Perspective: Lessons for Development Policy', *World Economics*, Vol. 7, No. 2, April–June 2006: http://citeseerx.ist.psu.edu/viewdoc/download?doi=10.1.1.516.4315&rep=rep1&type=pdf

17 Vikas Pota, 'Emerging Market Youth Embrace Liberal Globalism', 8 February 2017: https://www.ft.com/content/beb7ae08-ed48-11e6-930f-061b01e23655 (accessed 13 March 2017).

18 OECD, *Government at a Glance 2013*, OECD Publishing, 2013: http://www.oecd-ilibrary.org/governance/government-at-a-glance-2013_gov_glance-2013-en

19 Angus Maddison, 'Statistics on World Population, GDP and Per Capita GDP, 1–2008 AD': http://www.ggdc.net/maddison/oriindex.htm (accessed 8 February 2017).

20 Francis Fukuyama, 'The End of History?' *The National Interest*, summer 1989: https://ps321.community.uaf.edu/files/2012/10/Fukuyama-End-of-history-article.pdf

21 Charles Goodhart and Manoj Pradhan, 'Demographics Will Reverse Three Multi-decade Global Trends', BIS Working Papers No. 656, Bank for International Settlements, 2107: https://www.bis.org/publ/work656.htm

22 Data sources: 1980–2020 – IMF Database (2016 Economic Outlook), accessed 3 March 2017; 2050 – PwC GDP projections.

23 IMF Database (2017 Economic Outlook). Accessed 5 June 2017.

24 https://www.pwc.com/gx/en/world-2050/assets/pwc-world-in-2050-slide-pack-feb-2017.pdf

25 Saeed Shah, 'Pakistan's Middle Class Soars as Stability Returns', *Wall Street Journal*, 1 February 2017: https://www.wsj.com/articles/pakistans-middle-class-soars-as-stability-returns-1485945001 (accessed 6 February 2017).

26 World Bank, World Bank open data: http://data.worldbank.org/ (accessed 7 February 2017).

27 Homi Kharas, *The Emerging Middle Class in Developing Countries*, Working Paper No. 285, OECD Development

Centre: https://www.oecd.org/dev/44457738.pdf (accessed 7 February 2017).

28 'iMDB: The Case that has Riveted Malaysia', BBC News, 22 July 2016: http://www.bbc.com/news/world-asia-33447456

29 A. H. Roslan, 'Income Inequality, Poverty and Development Policy in Malaysia', a paper presented at the International Seminar on 'Poverty and Sustainable Development', 22–23 November 2001, organized by Université Montesquieu-Bordeaux IV and UNESCO-Paris, France (fully funded by UNESCO): http://ged.u-bordeaux4.fr/SBROSLAN.pdf (accessed 13 March 2017).

30 United Nations Statistics Division, Millennium Development Goals Database, 'Population Below National Poverty Line': http://data.un.org/Data.aspx?q=population+below+national+poverty+line%2c+total%2c+percentage&d=MDG&f=seriesRowID%3a581 (accessed 13 March 2017).

31 Asian Development Bank, 'The Rise of Asia's Middle Class', in *Key Indicators for Asia and the Pacific 2010*: https://www.adb.org/sites/default/files/publication/27726/special-chapter-02.pdf (accessed 13 March 2017).

32 Joyce Dargay, Dermot Gately and Martin Sommer, 'Vehicle Ownership and Income Growth, Worldwide: 1960–2030', January 2007: http://citeseerx.ist.psu.edu/viewdoc/download?doi=10.1.1.168.3895&rep=rep1&type=pdf (accessed 13 March 2017).

33 Source: World Bank, GDP per capita (constant 2010 US$).

34 Source: World Bank, school enrolment, tertiary, female (% gross).

35 Source: World Bank, GDP per capita (constant 2010 US$, 1981: 227 US$; 2015: 486 US$).

36 Kishore Mahbubani, 'The West and the Rest', *National Interest*, No. 28, summer 1992, pp. 3–12.

37 http://www.anth.ucsb.edu/faculty/stonich/classes/ anth130b/INTERNATIONAL%20TOURISM.pdf

38 http://www.e-unwto.org/doi/pdf/10.18111/9789284418145

39 Source: World Bank Database.

40 Source: World Bank data on mobile cellular subscriptions (per 100 people).

41 https://www.bloomberg.com/news/articles/2015-12-30/ india-becomes-second-phone-market-to-cross-1-billion- subscribers

42 'With 220mn Users, India is Now World's Second-biggest Smartphone Market', *The Hindu*, 3 February 2016: http:// www.thehindu.com/news/cities/mumbai/business/ with-220mn-users-india-is-now-worlds-secondbiggest- smartphone-market/article8186543.ece

43 https://www.ericsson.com/assets/local/mobility-report/ documents/2016/india-ericsson-mobility-report-june- 2016.pdf

44 Maddison, 'Statistics on World Population': http://www. ggdc.net/maddison/oriindex.htm (accessed 8 February 2017).

45 Kishore Mahbubani and Jeffery Sng, *The ASEAN Miracle: A Catalyst for Peace*, Singapore: NUS Press, 2017, p. 114.

46 Source: World Bank Database (June 2017).

47 Source: IMF World Economic Outlook (April 2017).

48 http://www.pewresearch.org/fact-tank/2017/04/06/why-muslims-are-the-worlds-fastest-growing-religious-group/

49 Ahmad Jibril, Twitter post, 13 January 2013: https://twitter.com/ahmadmusajibril/status/290455071479705601

50 Angus Roxburgh, letter, 'Nato is Misquoting Gorbachev', *Guardian*, 8 March 2015: https://www.theguardian.com/world/2015/mar/08/nato-is-misquoting-mikhail-gorbachev

51 Thomas L. Friedman, 'Why Putin Doesn't Respect Us', *New York Times*, 4 March 2014: https://www.nytimes.com/2014/03/05/opinion/friedman-why-putin-doesnt-respect-us.html?_r=0

52 http://www.spiegel.de/international/world/interview-with-henry-kissinger-on-state-of-global-politics-a-1002073.html

53 http://www.spiegel.de/international/world/interview-with-zbigniew-brzezinski-on-russia-and-ukraine-a-1041795.html

54 https://www.nbcnews.com/storyline/ukraine-crisis/mikhail-gorbachev-hails-crimea-result-happy-event-n55416

55 http://www.npr.org/2016/12/22/506625913/database-tracks-history-of-u-s-meddling-in-foreign-elections

56 Kishore Mahbubani, *Beyond the Age of Innocence: Rebuilding Trust between America and the World*, New York: Public Affairs, 2005, p. 144.

57 Kishore Mahbubani, *The Great Convergence: Asia, the West, and the Logic of One World*, New York: Public Affairs, 2013, pp. 3–4.

58 This was confirmed to the author by a senior American official.

59 Seamus Milne, 'Now the Truth Emerges: How the US Fuelled the Rise of Isis in Syria and Iraq', *Guardian*, 3 June 2015: https://www.theguardian.com/commentisfree/2015/jun/03/us-isis-syria-iraq

60 Charles Fisher, 'Southeast Asia: The Balkans of the Orient? A Study in Continuity and Change', *Geography*, Vol. 47, No. 4, 1962.

61 Mahbubani and Sng, *The ASEAN Miracle*.

62 Kevin Rudd, 'Myanmar's Rohingya Crisis Meets Reality', *New York Times*, 21 September 2017: https://www.nytimes.com/2017/09/21/opinion/myanmar-rohingya-aung-san-suu-kyi.html?mcubz=0&_r=0

63 https://www.poetryfoundation.org/poems/45362/locksley-hall

64 Patrick Moynihan, *A Dangerous Place*, Little, Brown, 1980, p. 247.

65 Maggie Farley, 'UN Resolutions Frequently Violated', *Los Angeles Times*, 17 October 2002: http://articles.latimes.com/2002/oct/17/world/fg-resolution17

66 https://usun.state.gov/remarks/7691

67 Shyam Saran, 'The Morning-after Principle', *Business Standard*, 10 June 2014: http://www.business-standard.com/article/opinion/shyam-saran-the-morning-after-principle-114061001300_1.html

68 https://in.news.yahoo.com/india-aligned-movement-post-brexit-100614501.html

69 Mahbubani, *The Great Convergence*, pp. 91–7.

70 http://www.margaretthatcher.org/document/106155

71 Berlin, 'The Question of Machiavelli'.

72 http://www.businessinsider.com/r-after-summits-with-trump-merkel-says-europe-must-take-fate-into-own-hands-2017-5/?IR=T

73 Source: World Bank, GDP per capita (constant 2010 US$), accessed 16 March 2017.

74 Hardeep Singh Puri, *Perilous Interventions: The Security Council and the Politics of Chaos*, Uttar Pradesh: HarperCollins India, 2016, p. 154.

75 Christopher Thornton, 'The Iran We Don't See', *The Atlantic*, 6 June 2012: https://www.theatlantic.com/international/archive/2012/06/the-iran-we-dont-see-a-tour-of-the-country-where-people-love-americans/258166/

76 Chas Freeman, 'Reimagining Great Power Relations', lecture at the Watson Institute for International and Public Affairs, Brown University, 9 March 2017: http://watson.brown.edu/files/watson/imce/people/fellows/freeman/ReimaginingGreatPowerRelations.pdf (accessed 23 March 2017).

77 Source: The Maddison Project.

78 Source: OECD projections.

79 Source: United Nations, medium fertility variant.

80 Mahbubani, *The Great Convergence*, pp. 239–40.

81 Kishore Mahbubani, 'When China Becomes Number One', *Horizons*, No. 4 (summer 2015): http://www.mahbubani.net/articles%20by%20dean/Horizons—Summer-2015—Issue-No.4-043-048.pdf

82 David B. Larter, 'Donald Trump Wants to Start the Biggest Navy Build-up in Decades', *Navy Times*, 15 November 2016: https://www.navytimes.com/articles/donald-trumps-navy-bigger-fleet-more-sailors-350-ships

83 http://yaleglobal.yale.edu/content/transcript-global-challenges

84 http://news.xinhuanet.com/english/2017-01/19/c_135994707.htm

85 https://www2.deloitte.com/global/en/pages/about-deloitte/articles/millennialsurvey.html

86 http://www.pewglobal.org/2014/10/09/emerging-and-developing-economies-much-more-optimistic-than-rich-countries-about-the-future/

87 http://oecdobserver.org/news/fullstory.php/aid/3681/An_emerging_middle_class.html

88 Nikil Saval, 'Globalisation: The Rise and Fall of an Idea that Swept the World', *Guardian*, 14 July 2017: https://www.theguardian.com/world/2017/jul/14/globalisation-the-rise-and-fall-of-an-idea-that-swept-the-world

89 https://www.forbes.com/sites/maggiemcgrath/2016/01/06/63-of-americans-dont-have-enough-savings-to-cover-a-500-emergency/#52ac4b464e0d

90 This was conveyed to the author in an email.

91 http://www.spiegel.de/international/world/trump-pulls-out-of-climate-deal-western-rift-deepens-a-1150486.html

Index